CO

BIF

OF THE INDIAN SUB-CONTINENT

including India, Pakistan, Bangladesh, Sri Lanka and Nepal

Written and illustrated by

Martin W. Woodcock

Designed by Hermann Heinzel

HarperCollins*Publishers*

HarperCollins Publishers
77-85 Fulham Palace Road
London
W6 8JB
United Kingdom

The HarperCollins Website address is:

www.**fire**and**water**.com

To the memory of the late J.R.S. (Roger) Holmes,
and of many happy days spent in the field. M.W.

First published 1980

05 04 03 02

16 15 14 13 12

Published in India in 2006

10 09 08 07 06 05 04 03 02 01

ISBN 13: 978 000 777 870 6
ISBN 10: 0 00 777 870 8

Colour reproduction by Adroit Photolitho Ltd., Birmingham
Filmsetting by Jolly& Barber Ltd., Rugby
Printed and bound at Thomson Press (India) Ltd.

Contents

Introduction		5
Podicipedidae	**Grebes**	16
Phalacrocoracidae	**Cormorants, Shags**	16
Anhingidae	**Darter**	16
Ardeidae	**Herons, Egrets, Bitterns**	18
Ciconiidae	**Storks**	22
Threskiornithidae	**Ibises, Spoonbill**	24
Phoenicopteridae	**Flamingos**	25
Anatidae	**Geese, Ducks**	26
Accipitridae	**Vultures, Kites, Harriers, Eagles, Buzzards, Hawk-Eagles, Hawks**	30
Falconidae	**Falcons**	36
Phasianidae	**Junglefowl, Peafowl**	38
	Monals, Tragopans, Pheasants	40
	Partridges, Spurfowl	42
	Partridges, Quails	44
Turnicidae	**Bustard-Quails**	45
Gruidae	**Cranes**	46
Otididae	**Bustards**	48
Rallidae	**Rails, Crakes, Coot, Moorhen**	50
Jacanidae	**Jacanas**	52
Rostratulidae	**Painted Snipe**	53
Charadriidae	**Plovers**	54
Scolopacidae	**Curlew, Snipe, Sandpipers**	56
Recurvirostridae	**Stilts**	58
Burhinidae	**Stone-Curlews**	58
Glareolidae	**Pratincoles, Coursers**	58
Pteroclididae	**Sandgrouse**	58
Laridae	**Gulls**	60
Sternidae	**Terns**	60
Columbidae	**Pigeons, Doves**	62
Psittacidae	**Parakeets, Lorikeets**	64
Cuculidae	**Cuckoos, Koel, Coucals**	66
Strigidae	**Owls**	68
Caprimulgidae	**Nightjars**	70
Apodidae	**Swifts**	70
Alcedinidae	**Kingfishers**	72
Meropidae	**Bee-Eaters**	72
Coraciidae	**Rollers**	74
Upupidae	**Hoopoe**	74

Bucerotidae	**Hornbills**	74
Capitonidae	**Barbets**	76
Picidae	**Woodpeckers**	76
Pittidae	**Pittas**	78
Alaudidae	**Larks**	78
Hirundinidae	**Swallows, Martins**	80
Motacillidae	**Pipits, Wagtails**	82
Campephagidae	**Cuckoo-Shrikes, Minivets**	84
Pycnonotidae	**Bulbuls**	86
Irenidae	**Ioras, Leafbirds, Fairy Bluebird**	88
Artamidae	**Swallow-Shrikes**	90
Laniidae	**Shrikes**	90
Muscicapidae	**Flycatchers**	92
Rhipiduridae	**Fantail Flycatchers**	92
Monarchidae	**Paradise Flycatchers**	92
Turdidae	**Thrushes, Chats, Robins**	94
Sylviidae	**Warblers**	98
Timaliidae	**Babblers, Laughing Thrushes**	100
Aegithalidae	**Longtailed Tits**	106
Paridae	**Tits**	106
Sittidae	**Nuthatches**	106
Certhiidae	**Creepers**	106
Dicaeidae	**Flowerpeckers**	108
Nectariniidae	**Sunbirds**	108
Zosteropidae	**White-Eyes**	108
Emberizidae	**Buntings**	110
Fringillidae	**Finches**	110
Estrildidae	**Avadavats, Munias**	112
Passeridae	**Sparrows**	114
Ploceidae	**Weavers**	114
Sturnidae	**Starlings, Mynas**	116
Oriolidae	**Orioles**	120
Corvidae	**Magpies, Treepies, Crows**	120
Dicruridae	**Drongos**	122
Index		170

For complete list of Indian Bird Families see Synopsis on p. 124.

Introduction

Few other areas of the world enjoy such a varied landscape as that of the Indian sub-continent, and the diversity of the scenery is fully reflected in the wonderfully rich bird-life, to which this book forms an introduction.

The area with which the book deals consists of India, Pakistan, Bangladesh, Sri Lanka, Nepal and Bhutan, and although this sounds rather extensive, the total of about 1.7 million square miles is considerably less than the 3.9m square miles of Europe (in its broadest sense, to the Ural mountains), and is only half the size of the United States of America, or Canada. Nevertheless, the total number of bird species recorded, at about 1250, is nearly twice the size of the European or North American list. Not surprisingly, there is a marked difference between the bird-life of the hot, dry, open plains in the west of the area and the steamy rain-forests of the eastern border, and between the snowy peaks and pine-woods of the Himalayas and the softer slopes of the hills in Sri Lanka, with their tea-gardens and picturesque waterfalls. All these places have their own characteristic birds, locally distributed species which only live in their particular environment, whether it be hill-forest, lowland jungle or desert. In contrast, many of the common birds of India are very widely distributed. It is important to try and get to know these species well, as there is still much of interest to be learnt about them, and once they can be recognised easily you will be able to identify the more uncommon birds.

This book has been designed to help you recognise the commoner birds of all types of habitat by illustrating a wide selection of them, in colour, in their natural surroundings. The simple supporting text aims to portray the character and habits of each species, rather than to describe the technicalities of plumage.

The bird-life in India

India and south-east Asia form the greater part of one of the world's six zoogeographical regions – natural provinces first described in the last century, within each of which the animal life is more closely related than it is to that of the others. Particularly characteristic bird families of this, the Oriental Region, include Pheasants, Leafbirds, Pittas and Flower-peckers. In the Indian sub-region, south of the Himalayas, the birds in many cases show close relationships with not only south-east Asian species, but, especially in the western areas, African birds. There are, of course, many indigenous species. Himalayan birds show much closer affinities with those of the Indo-Chinese sub-region, of which the mountain chain forms a long westward extension.

The total number of species recorded in the area covered by this book is about 1250, although many of these are rare or of limited range, and the birds treated in this book form the greater part of those likely to be seen anywhere in the area. Even to make the acquaintance of those shown in the pictures would take time, and quite a lot of travelling.

Although there are many species which give the Indian avifauna its own special character, most of the families are at least as richly represented in other areas, especially Africa, and some in tropical America. Examples of bird families which occur throughout the world's tropics include Pelicans, Ibises, Trogons, Barbets, Parrots and Cuckoos, while others such as birds of prey, owls, crows and the shorebirds have a world-wide distribution. Many of India's most characteristic birds are in families which only occur in the Old World tropics, such as Hornbills, Sunbirds, Bulbuls, Babblers and Cuckoo-Shrikes, while the Leafbirds or Fruitsuckers (p. 88) are confined to the Oriental Region. Families in which India is especially rich – often, incidentally, forest species – include Woodpeckers, Pigeons, Owls, Cuckoos, Pheasants, Drongos, Crows, Minivets, Babblers, Flycatchers and Warblers. In some families such as Babblers and Finches there are many more breeding species in the Himalayas than in the Indian sub-region. Many of the world's most impressive members of the Pheasant family come from the Himalayas, and the Peacock has been known from India since the Phoenicians brought them to the Pharaohs of Egypt. The birds of prey are well represented and often common, one of the best places to see them being around Delhi, especially in winter. The spectacular flocks of both breeding and wintering water-birds are one of the special attractions of India's jheels, and apart from the vast numbers of ducks and geese, cranes and wading birds which migrate south to India to seek their winter quarters, the numbers of smaller birds such as Thrushes, Flycatchers, Wagtails and Buntings are swelled by the arrival of more northerly breeders, which are often closely related to typical resident species.

Arranging and naming the birds

A brief note on how and why birds are classified may not be out of place here, and in practical terms has a bearing on the geographical variation noticeable in the plumage of many Indian birds. In order to show their relationships, birds (and all other animals and plants) are grouped in artificial but convenient categories such as Orders, Families, and Genera (plural of Genus) the last-named being used to group several individual species which are evidently very closely related – such as the little Munias (p. 112). The first of the two or three scientific names is the generic name, the second describes the species. Of all these categories, that of the species is the most objective and observable in nature, although not easy to define in simple terms. Briefly, it identifies a distinct population of individuals, which as regards reproduction are isolated from other populations by biological and behavioural patterns; so that a species may range over a huge area and live alongside and amongst other closely related species without losing its distinctness.

Within its total geographical range, however, a species may, as a result of local climatic or other influences, develop some permanent variation in plumage or structure, and where this variation is constant and

House Crows *Corvus splendens*, the race *zugmayeri* on the left.

confined to individuals of a restricted area, this group of individuals is ranked as a Sub-species, and given a third scientific name to mark the fact. Thus, the ordinary House Crow of most of India is called *Corvus splendens splendens*, while the well-marked, pale sub-species of north-west India and Pakistan is called *Corvus splendens zugmayeri*. Some groups of birds, such as the Wagtails (p. 82) have a series of sub-species in which males in breeding plumage are readily recognisable in the field. Subspecies in many other birds can only be identified by comparison in a museum collection.

Where the birds live

It is noticeable how most kinds of birds tend to keep to certain special surroundings, and it is not by chance that we find them there again and again. Many factors are at work in determining just where any given species can live and reproduce most successfully, and while some birds are much more adaptable than others, all are influenced by such things as their food requirements, the availability of nest-sites or song-posts, cover for roosting, and so forth. A convenient name for a bird's immediate and typical surroundings is 'habitat', and each type of habitat, whether it be hill forest, dense shrubberies, open countryside or marshland, has its own characteristic birds. Even quite closely related species, such as the Magpie Robin and the Shama, may occur in somewhat different habitats – one in gardens, parks and light woodland, the other skulking in deep forest or wooded ravines.

In the well watered parts of the plains, where there are jheels or lakes, and marshy fields, you will find herons, storks, rails and crakes, ducks, cormorants and other waterbirds. In the rank grass and reedbeds there may be coucals, weavers and many other small birds, while various birds of prey circle overhead. In drier open areas, thorn scrub or subdesert, such species as larks, chats, sandgrouse and bustards may be found. Around villages and towns you will be familiar with the pigeons, starlings and mynas, parakeets, sparrows, House Crows and other birds which thrive in cultivated areas, and bulbuls, doves, sunbirds and some of the warblers in parks and gardens. Drongos, shrikes and rollers like the more open areas, and the resonant calls of barbets are a familiar sound wherever there are trees. Some babblers are common and well-known in the plains, but this family reaches its greatest variety in the Himalayas, where the woods are also a paradise for flycatchers, warblers and many others, emphasising the fact that the woodland bird-life in the hills is quite well differentiated from that in the lowlands. Certain groups of birds become more diverse and noticeable, such as the minivets, cuckoos, flycatchers, tits and warblers, finches and buntings. Indeed, the variety of attractive species makes birding in the hills a most enjoy-

able pastime, with the added pleasure of walking in cooler conditions, often amidst beautiful scenery. Very often, though, the woodland birds are much more difficult to see than their open-country cousins, and a walk through wet evergreen hill-forest may reveal surprisingly few birds at first, until one is lucky enough to encounter a 'bird-wave' or hunting party. This is a well-known phenomenon, a twittering, active band of many species, keeping loose company as they search through the woods at all levels from the floor to the canopy. Often there are so many species that the flock has moved on before there is time to identify them all, or write their names down.

The distribution of birds in India

In the same way as birds living in one locality can be grouped by habitat, so on a country-wide scale is their distribution affected by climatic conditions and the physical geography of the land, which together determine the vegetation, and give each region its own characteristic appearance.

The Indian sub-continent is a peninsular roughly 2000km in length to the south of the great land-mass of Asia, being sharply demarcated along its northern border by the snowy arc of the Himalayas, which extend for a thousand miles along the edge of the Tibetan plateau. In the east, the monsoon which swells up into the Bay of Bengal in summer brings heavy rainfall, and allows luxuriant vegetation to clothe the eastern Himalayas, Assam, the valley of the Brahmaputra, and much of Bangladesh. The rainfall becomes progressively lighter further westwards, although even as far as central Nepal there is torrential rain in late summer on the southern slopes of the mountains. On the western borders, the Rajasthan desert – an offshoot of the great belt of arid lands which stretch from the Sahara to Mongolia – stands in marked contrast. The hard rocks of the Deccan, in peninsular India, have weathered into a broken and often hilly countryside, and are separated from the Himalayas by the great deposits washed down from the mountains by the Indo-Gangetic river systems. In the south-west of the peninsular, the beautiful hills of the western Ghats are well watered by the south-west monsoon, and form an isolated area of humid hill-forest.

For the purposes of this book, the area with which it deals can be divided into seven major regions, in each of which there is a more or less characteristic bird-life, although there are many local variations and exceptions. They are referred to in the text where necessary, sometimes just by their initial letters, to make a bird's distribution more clearly defined.

H **Himalayas** The bird-life is primarily Indo-Chinese in its affinities, although this is less marked in the west. The southern boundary follows the 1000km contour.

NW **North-West India & Pakistan** It includes the arid areas of the Punjab, Rajasthan and Kutch. Has many species which are common to the desert and sub-desert areas further west.

N **Northern India** The Gangetic plains. As this area extends to the 1000km contour it includes the forested zones along the Himalayan foothills, the *dun* and *bhabar*, and the swampy *terai* bordering the plains.

P **Peninsular India** or the Deccan, within which the next zone occurs, although in terms of bird-life it is well-differentiated.

SW **South-West India** The humid hills of Kerala and parts of Mysore and Madras are of particular interest, as they form a refuge for a

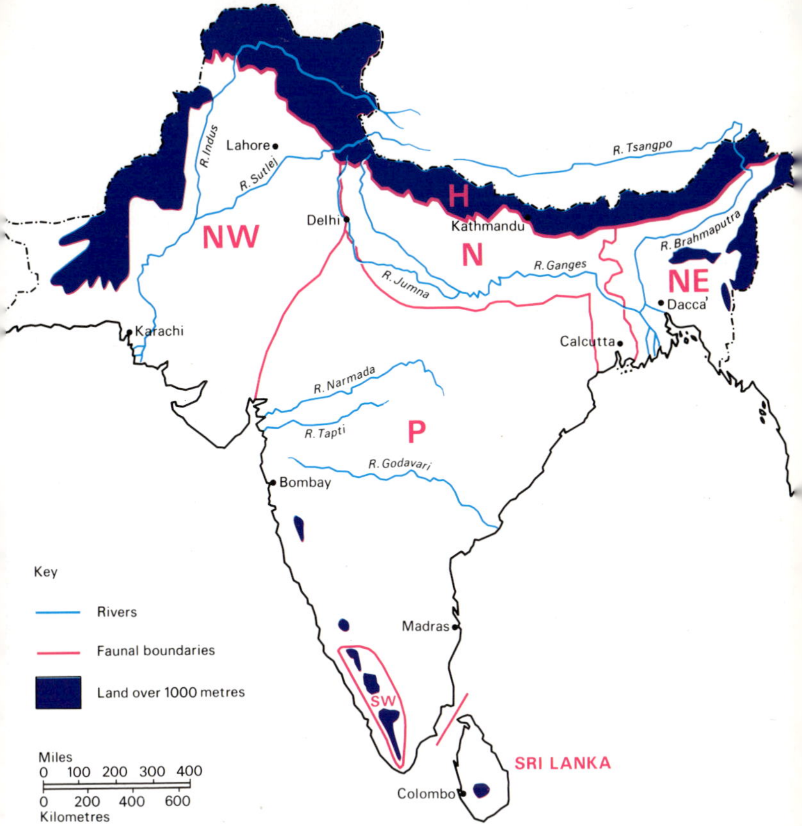

number of species which also occur in N.E. India and Burma. The term Western Ghats is used for the whole western flank of the Peninsular.

NE **North-East India & Bangladesh** Includes all the forest regions of Meghalaya, Mizoram and Nagaland, and the valley of the Brahmaputra. In the central and western parts the bird-life resembles that in N., but in the hills to the north and east the bird-life is mainly Indo-Chinese in character.

Sri Lanka The bird-life is similar to that of southern India, although it has some 21 species which do not occur anywhere else. Vultures are absent.

Some aspects of bird-life

Song, territory and courtship

The short, cheery whistle of a Red-whiskered Bulbul as it perches on a bush is a familiar sound, and probably attracts little attention. This song, although not as musical or complex as some, nevertheless has a special message to other Red-whiskered Bulbuls, for the cock uses it to advertise his presence to potential mates, and to mark out his territory, and all birds use song in this way. It is an important element of birds' breeding biology, and not to be confused with call-notes, which are mostly concerned with maintaining contact when feeding or in flight, or as alarm, threat or warning signals. The peak period for song marks the commencement of breeding for many small birds, and despite some exceptions and local variation, is well marked from roughly February to May, may be a month or so earlier in the south. Some birds use mechanically produced sounds i.e. bill clattering, territorially or in courtship, while true song ranges from the rich fluting of a Shama to the maddeningly repetitive calls of cuckoos. The staking-out of territory is an important preliminary to breeding, although different species vary greatly in their requirements, colonial nesters being content with a foot or two round the nest, while some species defend their territory fiercely. Territory is a complex subject in biological terms, and is by no means simply an area in which parent birds can be sure of finding sufficient food for their young. Courtship, which with many species often involves curious or beautiful display actions, serves a necessary biological function by ensuring that the birds concerned reach prime breeding condition simultaneously. Courtship displays are often designed to show off prominent features of the plumage – witness the Peacock's 'tail' – or may take the form of mutual preening or presenting food, as with parakeets and barbets. In colonial species, communal display supplements that of member pairs. An important function of display and song, which differ from species to species, is to ensure that mating only occurs between birds of the same species.

Breeding habits, nests and eggs

The breeding season in sub-tropical areas is not so concentrated in time as it is in more temperate latitudes, and in India falls into three fairly well-defined periods, although there is much variation, and in the south and the plains these periods are more extended than they are in the hills. From about October to March, most of the larger birds of prey and the big owls are nesting, while from March to May there is a peak of activity for many common birds, and most Himalayan and hill birds, although the really high-altitude nesters start late, in June and July. In the rains, whenever they occur from district to district, the waterbirds, storks, and small birds such as weavers, munias and warblers breed, taking advantage of the burgeoning aquatic and insect life, although riverine birds such as pratincoles, plovers and terns have to nest before the monsoon swells water levels. Most species need to build new nests each year, and the variety, especially amongst small birds, is wonderful, ranging from the delicate, suspended purse of fibres and cobwebs of a sunbird to the Pitta's domed structure of twigs and grass. The expertise of Tailorbirds at stitching leaves together is well-known. Many ground-nesting birds are content with a simple scrape in the earth. Nesting habits, too, vary greatly, and are of absorbing interest. Hornbills are unique in walling-up the female in the nest-hole, leaving a slit through which she is fed by the male, while at the other extreme some babblers nest communally, several hens laying in one nest, while up to six adults attend the chicks. Eggs differ enormously in colour and markings, although often those which are laid in holes are white, while many of the ground-nesting birds such as plovers and terns have protectively coloured eggs. Texture and structure in eggs are variable too; the parasitic cuckoos, for example, lay relatively small eggs with extra thick shells, presumably to protect them when they are dropped in other bird's nests. A clutch comprises all the eggs laid by a hen for a single nesting; most small birds, also ducks and gamebirds, do not start incubating until the last egg is laid. Most larger birds, also swifts, start with the first egg, so the chicks hatch at different times. Song-bird chicks are born naked and have to be brooded and fed, while those of gamebirds, for instance, are feathered and soon active.

Feeding, moult and migration

The type of food a bird eats has much to do with both its habitat and structure, especially the beak, legs and feet. Sunbirds, for instance, have delicate, curved bills for flower-probing, and short, weak legs and feet. At the other extreme, herons have long legs for wading in the water where they spear fish with their heavy, pointed bills. Many other examples of this type of adaptation can be seen. Small differences in diet, though, mean that many species can forage profitably in the same small area – even in a single tree – each exploiting a particular segment of the vegetation.

When the breeding season is over, it is often noticeable how the parent birds have become ragged and tatty, their feathers worn and broken. This is because the process of moulting – the shedding and renewal of feathers – has been delayed until parental duties are finished. Feathers are not moulted haphazardly, and indeed the flight feathers are shed in a fixed order, which can vary from species to species. Corresponding feathers on each wing are moulted simultaneously to maintain flight balance, generally once a year, while body feathers may be moulted twice a year or more. Plumage pattern and markings can also change through wear of the feather tips, where incidentally black pigmentation is noticeably wear-resistant.

The Indian sub-continent is host in winter to a multitude of birds which have nested further north in Asia, and migrate over the mountains to seek congenial winter quarters. Some species, such as Rosy Starlings, migrate in large flocks over quite narrow routes, but most migration is less obvious, and often takes place at night. Lying at the southern end of a great land-mass, India and especially Sri Lanka do not have summer visitors on the scale of more northerly lands, although many birds return to breeding areas from which they have wandered in the off-season, and there is regular migration within the area by such birds as Pittas and Golden Orioles.

How to use the book

By reading the text through carefully, and studying the illustrations, you should be able to gain some idea of which birds, and groups of birds, are likely to occur in the various types of country or habitat you are able to visit. Half the battle in bird identification is in knowing what to expect in a given area or season. A basic knowledge of habits will also help you to learn the birds more quickly, but remember that the odds are on seeing common rather than rare birds and that it is by no means always possible, even for experts, to identify every bird.

It is important to visit as many different types of habitat as you can, and equally to study one area, if you can, through the year. You will need little equipment beyond a reference book, a cheap notebook, and perhaps a pair of binoculars, which are essential for serious birding, although much useful observation can be done without them. Songs and calls help to locate many species, especially in thick cover, and the only way to learn the calls is the hard way, by constant tracking down and memorizing. When in woodland, move slowly and quietly – sitting still, insects permitting, is often the best course. You will soon find the most productive places – sun-splashed glades or fruiting trees in the woods, or jheels, rivers or marshes. It is well worth keeping one's own notes, as the act of writing things down fixes them better in the memory and sharpens observation. It is essential to make as full notes as possible about any bird you cannot at once identify.

DABCHICK *Tachybaptus ruficollis.* 23cm. The smallest of the swimming birds; a constant diver, disappearing abruptly and neatly when alarmed or feeding. Finds most of its food under water, and has well-waterproofed and rather silky plumage. Like other grebes, it has the curious habit of swallowing its own feathers, apparently to aid digestion. The nest is a floating pad of waterweed. Found on tanks, jheels, ponds or even ditches in the plains and lower hills throughout the area. Often solitary or in small groups, or in larger flocks in winter.

GREAT CORMORANT *Phalacrocorax carbo.* 82cm. Although less restricted to lowland waters, it is neither as numerous nor as gregarious as its smaller relatives. Cormorants hunt fish by diving from the surface, often making a little upward jump first. The stiff tail is used as a rudder under water. Despite being aquatic birds, their plumage is coarse and not particularly water-resistant, and much time is spent on sandbanks or tree-stumps with the wings held out to dry. It occurs throughout the area, breeding in large waterside colonies.

INDIAN SHAG *P. fuscicollis.* 62cm. Often confused with the Little Cormorant, it is nearly as abundant. It is an active swimmer and diver, and very sociable. Found throughout the area in the lowlands.

DARTER *Anhinga rufa.* 90cm. The most highly specialised of underwater fishers. Swims with the body submerged, the small head and sinuous neck resulting in its other name of Snakebird. Fish are speared with a sudden straightening of the neck, the curiously formed neckbones acting like a trigger. Darters are less sociable than Cormorants, and often seen singly. Strong fliers, frequently soaring, the long tail fanned out. Breeds colonially in the lowlands.

LITTLE CORMORANT *P. niger.* 50cm. The most abundant of its ▷ family, gathering in huge numbers at some waterside breeding colonies. Also nests in trees in village compounds some way from water. Constantly consorts with the Shag in a jostling, splashing throng to harry shoals of fish. It flies strongly, the neck outstretched, the wingbeats interspersed with short glides. The nestlings are ugly and scrawny, and noisily pester their parents to regurgitate the food in their crops, plunging their bills in to feed.

display
LITTLE EGRET
non-
breed
breeding
CATTLE EGRET
imm
adult
GREY HERON

LITTLE EGRET *Egretta garzetta.* 62cm. The fashion for wearing "aigrettes" – the beautiful plumes grown by egrets in the breeding season – nearly led to its extinction in certain areas some years ago. Happily, however, many remain in India to adorn the marshes and jheels where they stalk about after fish, frogs and insects. When feeding in shallow water they sometimes dash about wildly, probably to disturb their prey. They fly with slow, steady flaps, the neck well tucked in, and nest in large waterside colonies with other species. Little Egrets are resident throughout the area.

CATTLE EGRET *Bubulcus ibis.* 50cm. Constant attendance on grazing animals earns this small heron its name, and it is less confined to the waterside than its relatives, flocks sometimes being found in dry grassland or ploughed fields. It perches readily on cattle, buffaloes or other large animals, and rids them of leeches, as well as feeding on the insect life they disturb from underfoot. Breeding colonies are often in large trees in or around villages, well away from water in some places, and the birds have favourite roosting trees, shared with other species. They are resident throughout the area in the plains and lower hills.

GREY HERON *Ardea cinerea.* 95cm. A more solitary bird away from its breeding colonies than the egrets, it is nevertheless a familiar figure whether by lowland pond or hill stream. A skilled and patient fisherman, its gawky shape is distinctive when poised with neck outstretched at the water's edge, or when beating slowly across the sky on broad wings. The large stick nests are usually placed in tall trees, or by the water in reedbeds or mangroves. The scraggy nestlings are fed on regurgitated food, which they solicit by tugging at the parent's bill.

REEF HERON *Egretta gularis.* 62cm. Essentially a coastal species, it is markedly more common in Pakistan and western India than on the Madras coast. It is commonly seen in an all-white plumage, when it resembles a Little Egret, although the habitat is a clue to its identity. A rather solitary but active fisher from reefs or tidal mud. The nesting colonies are in mangroves. ▷

NIGHT HERON *Nycticorax nycticorax.* 58cm. Although often as abundant as the more conspicuous egrets, it is much less active in the daytime, and consequently may be less noticed. At dusk, the birds flap slowly out of the trees or bushes where they have been dozing quietly all day, dispersing to marshy fields and ponds to feed on small fish, frogs and insects. Nests colonially, sometimes in association with other species, in dense bushes or leafy trees, usually near water. Widely distributed at up to about 2,000m.

YELLOW BITTERN *Ixobrychus* ◁ *sinensis.* 35cm. Smallest of all the herons, this bird frequents large reedbeds and lush waterside vegetation, where it may sometimes be seen, clambering about among the thicker stems. Although not really shy, its haunts make it difficult to watch. Also, it tends to be more active by night. When alarmed, bitterns have a characteristic habit of standing motionless, neck stretched up and bill pointing skywards, so that from the front the plumage pattern resembles dead reeds. Widely distributed in the lowlands.

PADDYBIRD *Ardeola grayii.* 45cm. One of the most familiar birds in India, it can be seen by every pool, ditch or swamp. The typical hunched figure of the standing bird is transformed in flight, when the white wings flash into view. Dowdy and inconspicuous by the water, it is not a shy bird, feeding unafraid around the village pond, or waiting patiently to spear a fish or frog. Often seen singly, but sociable at roosts, nesting among other herons. Widely distributed at up to about 1700m.

LITTLE GREEN HERON *Butorides striatus.* 45cm. A lover of jungle streams or pools overshadowed by thick vegetation, or tangled swamps and mangroves. Rather shy and solitary, and partly nocturnal. When disturbed at the waterside flies up into the trees, the wings looking large for the small, slender body. Unusual among the herons in breeding solitarily, often in waterside bushes, although so quiet and secretive that a pair may nest close to a village and remain undetected. Widely but rather thinly distributed in the lowlands.

OPENBILL STORK *Anastomus oscitans.* 80cm. The commonest stork in India, and a highly gregarious bird, nesting in large colonies. Like all storks, it is a powerful flier, soaring at great heights, and can plunge earthwards in a swaying, tumbling but controlled dive. Courtship is marked by a ritualised swinging up and down of the head and neck. The curious bill is an adaptation enabling the bird to grasp the large fresh-water snails on which it feeds. It is widely distributed.

PAINTED STORK *Ibis leucocephalus.* 100cm. A familiar sight at inland waters in the plains, it is mainly a fish-eater, and often wades along with the half-opened bill ploughing through the water. Usually seen in small numbers, except at the teeming breeding colonies.

WHITE STORK *Ciconia ciconia.* 90cm. A winter visitor to India, rarer in the south than the north and west. Usually in small parties by jheels, marshes or wet fields where a variety of food is taken, including frogs and grasshoppers. Migrating flocks make use of rising hot air currents – "thermals" – to soar and gain height, and are then a conspicuous sight.

WHITE-NECKED STORK *C. episcopus.* 90cm. Often seen singly or in small parties, it is a fairly common resident in the lowlands. It haunts irrigated fields, small marshes and wet grassland, and is a solitary nester, building in a large tree. A strong flier, it often soars with other storks and vultures.

ADJUTANT STORK *Leptopilos dubius.* 150cm. This is an impressive bird, whether stalking over marshland, or soaring on its huge wings, often in company with vultures. An avid scavenger of any refuse, offal or carcase, it also feeds on fish, frogs or snakes. The function of the curious inflatable neck pouch is not known, although it is certainly not capable of storing food as might be imagined. Nesting in Bangladesh and Assam, this stork wanders widely across northern India.

SPOONBILL *Platalea leucorodia.* 85cm. The peculiar bill, flattened and broadened at the tip, is adapted for feeding in shallow water. As the bird moves forward, the bill is swept from side to side, sifting the bottom for small aquatic animals. Sociable but rather inactive. Spoonbills spend much of the day standing around in marshes and swamps. They breed colonially with herons and cormorants, and occur throughout the area.

GLOSSY IBIS *Plegadis falcinellus.* 55cm. A close-up view reveals the shining green and copper tints in the plumage, which commonly looks black at a distance. Often in parties, it frequents jheels or flooded fields in lowlands throughout the area, but is rare in the south and Sri Lanka. Breeds alongside other water birds, the small stick nest being built in trees. In flight the neck is stretched out, and the rather pointed wings are beaten rapidly, interspersed with glides.

WHITE IBIS *Threskiornis melanocephalus.* 75cm. Perhaps a commoner bird than the Glossy Ibis, and rather more generally distributed. It has the rare distinction among waterside birds in that the head and neck are bare. It nests in trees, often with other species. The chicks are fed by regurgitation.

◁ **GREATER FLAMINGO** *Phoenicopterus ruber.* 130cm. Like the Spoonbill, it has a specialised beak for sifting small animal matter from shallow water, but does this by curving the long neck so that the bill is upside down, pointing back at the feet, and moving it from side to side. The only breeding area known in India is in Kutch, where many birds congregate to build their mud-pie nests on the salt flats. In winter the birds may be seen on jheels throughout the area; rarely in the east.

◁ **BLACK IBIS** *Pseudibis papillosa.* 68cm. Not a gregarious bird, it haunts dry grassy areas or stubble fields. It generally nests solitarily, often in a tall tree, and feeds on lizards, snakes, beetles and scorpions. It is found across northern and central India.

BAR-HEADED GOOSE *Anser indicus.* 75cm. Common in winter in northern and central India, but rarer further south. Usually in large, wary flocks on jheels or by rivers, it is frequently shot owing to its depredations on crops. The flocks fly in a long, strung-out V formation, and the wild musical honking is best heard when the birds are flighting to or from their feeding grounds. It is known to fly at very high altitudes when on migration over the Himalayas.

NAKTA or COMB DUCK *Sarkidiornis melanotos.* 76cm. This curious and ungainly-looking duck is in fact a better walker and percher than most ducks, and nests in holes or hollows in trees, usually in woodland near water. It is rare or absent from most of western India, Pakistan and Sri Lanka. Generally in small parties, it is a strong flier, and grazes on crops and grasses in the fields and marshes.

WHISTLING DUCK *Dendrocygna javanica.* 42cm. Also a tree-nesting species, this duck frequents similar well-wooded districts throughout the area, being partial to weed-covered village ponds or jheels. It is more active, and often feeds, at night, except where it is left undisturbed. The hoarse, wheezy call is uttered in flight, when it flaps in rather laboured fashion on rounded wings. Usually in small groups, but sometimes in large flocks in winter, notably at the Alipore Zoo in Calcutta.

COTTON TEAL *Nettapus coromandelianus.* 33cm. The smallest duck in the world; it is widespread in the better watered areas of India except in the south-west, although nowhere really abundant. Usually in pairs or small flocks on weedy tanks or jheels, where it feeds on water plants. The nest is placed in a hole in a tree. Although not adept at either diving or walking, it flies fast and well.

adult
imm
BAR-HEADED GOOSE
♀
♂
NAKTA
WHISTLING
DUCK
COTTON
TEAL
♂
♀

SPOTBILL *Anas poecilorhyncha.* 60cm. Only this bird, and to a rather less extent the three ducks on p. 27 are widespread breeders in our area, most species being winter visitors. Fast, strong fliers with necks outstretched, Spotbills are typical of the dabbling ducks, which "up-end" in shallow water and graze in marshes or crops. Unusually, though, the sexes are alike; in most species the drakes moult into a duck-like plumage briefly after the breeding season. Found in pairs or groups rather thinly though the lowlands and foothills on tanks, ponds and jheels.

COMMON TEAL *A. crecca.* 37cm. Abundant throughout the area in winter, this is a very agile duck, twisting and turning in flight and springing off the water with characteristic dash when alarmed. The drake looks rather dark at a distance, a closer view revealing the attractive colouring. Like other dabblers, it feeds mainly on vegetable matter. Sometimes seen in huge flocks, but usually occurs in much smaller parties.

PINTAIL *A. acuta.* 60cm. Alert and wary, this is one of the most elegant of the ducks, the long pointed tail being distinctive both at rest and when flying. Often feeds at night, especially where much disturbed. It is a good walker, holding the long neck erect, and the wings make a distinct hissing noise in flight. Common in winter throughout the area on jheels or coastal waters.

BRAHMINY DUCK *Tadorna ferruginea.* 65cm. A handsome, rather goose-like duck, breeding in the desolate lake-studded areas of the Tibetan plateau. Winters widely across India, seeking out clean open stretches of water with sandy or shingly shores and spits. Generally shy, it is usually seen in small groups. The clanging call is sufficiently well-known to have won the bird a place in Indian folk-lore.

FERRUGINOUS DUCK *Aythya nyroca.* 40cm. This dark little species is typical of the diving ducks, which are rather tubby, barrel-shaped fish-eaters, diving below the surface for food. They are poor walkers, the legs being set far back on the body. Found on lakes or jheels with large open stretches of open water amongst the vegetation. Breeding in Kashmir, it winters to north and central India, becoming rarer in the south and east.

SPOTBILL
♂
♀
TEAL
♀
♂
PINTAIL
♀
BRAHMINY
DUCK
♂
♀
♂
FERRUGINOUS
DUCK

LAMMERGEYER *Gypaetus barbatus.* 100cm. A magnificent bird, usually seen floating along a mountainside on wings which may measure nine feet across. It is unique in feeding on bones, carrying them high in the air to drop them on rocks, then swooping down to pick out the marrow. It also feeds at carcases and around village rubbish dumps. Haunts the mountain ranges from Pakistan to Bhutan, nesting on inaccessible cliffs.

WHITE-BACKED VULTURE *Gyps bengalensis.* 90cm. Generally the commonest of the vultures in the jostling, flapping rabble round a carcase. Often sits around in trees or on buildings, looking a heavy, unkempt bird at rest, but like all vultures a wonderful flier. Although a disgusting feeder, often entering a carcase to pull out the entrails, it misses no opportunity to bathe when water is available. Found throughout the area except Sri Lanka.

KING VULTURE *Torgos calvus.* 82cm. A striking-looking bird, thinly distributed throughout the area except Sri Lanka. Noticeably less sociable both at carcases and when breeding than the two commoner large vultures, and often seen singly. Despite its powerful bill, it is not a dominant species at a mixed feeding group, but stands round the edge, awaiting a clear moment to snatch a morsel. The large nest is built in a tall tree.

LONG-BILLED VULTURE *G. indicus.* 90cm. In some areas, particularly the Himalayan foothills and Bangladesh, it is commoner than the White-backed, but is absent from the extreme south and Sri Lanka. Nests on cliff precipices or old forts, often in small colonies. This bird is just as aggressive when feeding as the White-backed, and has even been found trapped in a carcase.

SCAVENGER VULTURE *Neophron percnopterus.* 65cm. This small, bedraggled-looking vulture is common throughout the area, except Bangladesh and Sri Lanka. It is a bird of repulsive habits, although as a devourer of every kind of garbage it may render some beneficial effects in the absence of sanitation. Like an unkempt fowl when on the ground, where it waddles easily, it is much more impressive in flight. The stick nest is placed in a tree or on a building, and two beautifully marked eggs are laid.

LAMMERGEYER
KING VULTURE
WHITE-BACKED VULTURE
LONG-BILLED VULTURE
imm
SCAVENGER VULTURE
adult

BLACK-WINGED KITE *Elanus caeruleus.* 33cm. This elegant and sociable little kite is widely distributed, frequenting low-lying grasslands, cultivation or light jungle. It beats slowly over a field, gliding with wings held in a shallow V, or hovers to inspect a small area more closely. When perched, it has a trick of drooping the wings and cocking the tail up.

BRAHMINY KITE *Haliastur indus.* 48cm. A familiar scavenger by harbours, rivers, lakes or jheels, it is very widely distributed in southern Asia. Although not such an adroit flier as the longer-tailed Pariah Kite, it can nevertheless snatch fish from the surface of the water, and catch large insects in flight.

PARIAH KITE *Milvus migrans.* 65cm. One of the most noticeable birds in the sub-continent, this abundant and successful scavenger can be seen soaring or flapping around villages and towns at all times. Avoiding only dense forests, it is everywhere parasitic on man, and boldly swoops down to snatch food from the busiest street or market. The flight is easy and graceful, on angled and flexing wings, the tail being constantly used as a rudder.

PALLID HARRIER *Circus macrourus.* 48cm. Haunts open countryside, whether stony fields or lush grassland. Usually seen quartering the ground methodically at no great height, alternately flapping and floating on up-turned wings, now gaining and then losing height. An unsuspecting frog or lizard is pounced on from a few feet above before escape is possible, but agile prey is not pursued. It is a winter visitor.

MARSH HARRIER *C. aeruginosus.* 55cm. More addicted to wet pastures, swamps and reedbeds than the Pallid Harrier. In the dark brown plumage it can be confused with a Pariah Kite, but its habit of quartering low over the reeds is distinctive. On occasion, however, it likes to soar high in the air, the primaries splayed out like fingers. It has earned a reputation for robbing the sportsman, as it quickly pounces on a wounded duck or snipe. It is a winter visitor.

BLACK-WINGED KITE
adult
BRAHMINY KITE
imm
PARIAH KITE
♀
PALLID HARRIER
imm
MARSH HARRIER

CRESTED
SERPENT-EAGLE
imm
STEPPE
EAGLE
WHITE-EYED
BUZZARD
TAWNY
EAGLE

PALLAS'S FISH-EAGLE *Haliaeetus leucoryphus.* 85cm. This fine eagle is commonly seen around lakes, rivers or jheels, often sitting on a sandbank or post. A powerful bird, it can kill large fish or other prey, although sometimes eating carrion, or robbing other birds. It creates havoc at nesting colonies of herons or cormorants. It has a loud barking call which can be heard at great distances, and is found across northern India, from Pakistan to Assam.

CRESTED SERPENT-EAGLE *Spilornis cheela.* 70cm. The loose crest, which can be erected like a ruff, gives the bird a large-headed appearance at rest, but it is generally seen soaring over forests, when the under-wing pattern is striking. It feeds to a large extent on reptiles, also taking frogs and insects, and is widely distributed throughout the plains and hills, in wooded areas.

WHITE-EYED BUZZARD *Butastur teesa.* 42cm. A rather dull and sluggish bird, it likes to spend a lot of time sitting on telegraph posts or bushes while on the look-out for a meal. It frequents open country, light scrub or cultivation in lowlands and foothills; absent in Sri Lanka.

TAWNY EAGLE *Aquila rapax.* 70cm. The drier plains of northern and central India are the home of this common and heavily-built eagle. Usually seen perched in a bush or tree, it is a fine flier, soaring round in wide circles. Although often feeding on carrion, it readily kills small mammals and birds, and robs other birds of prey. Closely related is the Steppe Eagle, *A. nipalensis*, a winter visitor to the Himalayas and northern India, often seen in the immature plumage shown.

CRESTED HAWK-EAGLE *Spizaetus cirrhatus.* 70cm. The commonest of a group of similar-looking and rapacious eagles, it is a bird of forests or well-wooded country. Resembles the larger hawks, as it has a long tail and rather rounded wings, designed for rapid and agile flight under the forest canopy. It is rarely seen soaring. A noisy bird with a shrill cry, it has earned a reputation for stealing poultry, although generally feeding on small animals and birds. Found in the Himalayas, N.E. and Peninsular India and Sri Lanka.

SHIKRA *Accipiter badius.* 33cm. One of the commonest small hawks, it frequents well-wooded country, but not heavy forest, throughout the area. The flight is typical, several stiff flaps being followed by a short glide, the bird often swooping upwards as it prepares to alight in a tree.

REDHEADED MERLIN *Falco chicquera.* 33cm. Occurs throughout the area, except in Sri Lanka, in open or lightly wooded country. A courageous and fierce predator, and has a fast and dashing flight on pointed wings, feeding mostly on small birds. Recorded as often hunting in pairs, one bird flushing the prey from cover while the other waits to pounce.

KESTREL *F. tinnunculus.* 35cm. A common winter visitor throughout the area, and also resident in the Himalayas, S.W. India and Sri Lanka, in open or hilly country. Best known for its habit of hovering on flickering wings as it scans the ground for mice and insects. In normal flight is less powerful than the other falcons, the pointed wings beating shallowly. It nests on a ledge of a cliff or ruin.

LAGGAR FALCON *F. jugger.* 45cm. Commonest of the large falcons, and found in open country, cultivation or near-desert in the plains or foothills, except in the south and Sri Lanka. Often seen in pairs, it preys on small birds and mammals, and is a powerful flier.

SHIKRA
RED-HEADED
MERLIN
KESTREL
♀
♂
LAGGAR

♀
♂
♂
♀
RED
JUNGLEFOWL

GREY JUNGLEFOWL *Gallus sonneratii.* 70cm. Found in the central, western and southern parts of Peninsular India. It is very shy, and most likely to be seen at dawn on some jungle track, when single birds or small parties venture out cautiously to feed. Haunts forests and bamboo groves on hill slopes up to 1700m. Like most pheasants, it roosts in trees, and passes the heat of the day quietly in the undergrowth.

RED JUNGLEFOWL *G. gallus.* 65cm. The ancestor of all domestic poultry. In the wild, a shy inhabitant of bamboo and scrubby jungle, often near cultivation. It occurs over a wide area of north-east Peninsular India to Assam and in the Himalayas west to Kashmir, at up to about 1700m. A gregarious bird, and probably the most abundant member of the pheasant family; often, however, the birds' presence is only given away by the cock's crowing – very similar to that of a domestic fowl. When alarmed, runs rapidly for cover, the neck stretched out and tail depressed.

PEAFOWL *Pavo cristatus.* Male up to 210cm. Female 100cm. Where found in a wild state, this familiar gamebird haunts fairly thick, well-watered jungle in hilly country, throughout India and Sri Lanka. It is extremely shy and difficult to see; having excellent sight and hearing and constantly on the alert, a flock will quickly disappear at the first suspicion of danger. Although it looks cumbersome, the cock's "tail" does not inconvenience him whether running through vegetation or beating up into his roost; when walking it is carried just off the ground.

▽

♀
♂
♂
♀
SATYR
TRAGOPAN
♂
♀
KALIJ
PHEASANT

◁ **MONAL** *Lophophorus impejanus.* 70cm. This magnificent pheasant haunts the upper valleys of the Himalayas, rarely descending below about 2000m, even in winter. It is especially partial to the rocky alpine meadows where they are intersected by clumps of fir or rhododendron, and here the birds dig for bulbs and roots with their powerful beaks. They tend to keep in small parties, and are very shy, shooting off downhill when disturbed, with a loud whistling call. When displaying, the cock fans and raises his rufous tail, droops his wings to reveal the white back-patch, and fluffs out the brilliant iridescent neck feathers.

SATYR TRAGOPAN *Tragopan satyra.* 70cm. Tragopans are noteworthy for the brilliantly coloured and patterned inflatable throat lappet of the males, used when displaying; the colours and pattern vary from species to species. The Satyr Tragopan occurs in the higher forests in the Himalayas, moving lower in winter. It is difficult to see or watch, being very shy, but sometimes feeds out on the open turf where there is nearby cover, at dawn or in the evening. Much time, however, is spent scratching about in the bamboo and rhododendron undergrowth in the ravines and gulleys. Tragopans have a loud, raucous alarm-note, and a booming or bleating call.

KALIJ PHEASANT *Lophura leucomelana.* 70cm. The most familiar of the Himalayan pheasants, being less restricted to high or remote areas than most others. It occurs from Kashmir to Bhutan and Assam in several different races, being distinguished by the amount of white in the plumage. The white-crested bird illustrated is from the west Himalayas, the darker bird from Nepal. It is fond of the thick undergrowth of jungle ravines, but also frequents cultivation around hill villages. It is more active at dawn and dusk, and can then sometimes be seen in clearings or along tracks. Small parties keep in touch with a low clucking call, and the cock makes a deep drumming noise when displaying by vibrating his wings rapidly.

KALIJ PHEASANT
White crested race

♀
♂
BLACK PARTRIDGE
PAINTED PARTRIDGE
COMMON HILL-PARTRIDGE
GREY PARTRIDGE
♀
♂
RED SPURFOWL

BLACK PARTRIDGE *Francolinus francolinus.* 33cm. Found along the Himalayan foothills and across a wide belt of northern India. A bird of grassland and cultivation, often near rivers in the plains, and of scrub-jungle and tea-gardens. It attracts attention by its remarkable creaking and repetitive call, which the cock makes while perched on a low tree, mound or anthill. Usually flushed singly or in small covies, the birds whirr away noisily on bowed wings, with the typical gamebird flap and glide flight.

PAINTED PARTRIDGE *F. pictus.* 30cm. Occurring throughout most of the Peninsular and in Sri Lanka, this species is evidently closely related to the Black Partridge, as they are known to hybridise in some areas. Although particularly addicted to perching, it is a secretive bird and a great believer in crouching motionless to escape detection, flying up only as a last resort. Found in dry, thin jungle or areas of abandoned cultivation, and most active at dawn and dusk, when they may be watched scratching about on the ground for seeds and insects.

COMMON HILL-PARTRIDGE *Arborophila torqueola.* 28cm. A hill bird from Kashmir to Assam, haunting densely forested ravines in broken rocky country. Often going about in small parties, they are very vocal, keeping up a succession of low, whistling notes. Although unwilling fliers, they are quite strong on the wing, and not as noisy as lowland partridges. Active throughout the day, they enjoy basking in the patches of sunlight on the hillside amongst the moss and brambles and profusion of flowers typical of such places.

GREY PARTRIDGE *F. pondicerianus.* 33cm. Found throughout most of India and Sri Lanka, it is a bird of dry open ground and light jungle. The cocks are well-known for their pugnacity, and their loud, triple challenging call is a familiar sound. Trapping has reduced the number of these birds drastically in some areas. They are swift runners, and will try to escape danger by trusting their legs rather than flying; they usually run some distance on landing after being forced into the air.

RED SPURFOWL *Galloperdix spadicea.* 37cm. Spurfowl have resemblances to both partridges and junglefowl, though their haunts and habits are those of the latter. They have large multiple spurs behind the tarsus, old males sometimes having four on each leg, and females up to two. Frequenting thick scrub or bamboo jungle in rocky, broken and hilly country, they occur over most of the central and southern peninsular. Shy and skulking, usually going about in small parties, they are most likely to be seen in early morning or evening, when they come out into the more open areas of the forest to feed. Although fast runners, they are poor fliers. They have a loud cackling call.

COMMON QUAIL *Coturnix coturnix.* 20cm. A breeding bird of northern and western India, and a numerous and widely distributed winter visitor. In spring, large numbers migrate through the north-west on their way to Europe and Russia. Usually found in scattered flocks, sometimes very large; the liquid triple whistle is a sure guide to their presence. When put up out of the crops or meadows where they have been feeding, they fly low, straight and fast on whirring wings.

RAIN QUAIL *C. coromandelica*. 17cm. A resident throughout India in the plains and lower hills, occasionally straggling to Sri Lanka. It is usually found singly or in pairs, and is a bird of open country and cultivation, sometimes around villages or even in gardens. The call is a double whistle. The birds wander in response to weather conditions, moving out of dry areas in the hot weather to seek shelter in grassland or bush.

◁ **CHUKAR** *Alectoris chukar.* 37cm. The bare, arid hillsides of Pakistan, the Punjab and the western Himalayas are the home of this large partridge. A stout, pale, fast-running bird, most often seen in small covies. When put up the birds shoot off downhill, the rounded arched wings whirring. Very hardy birds, able to withstand equally well the great heat of the Baluchi hills or the cold of the high Himalayas, where they ascend to over 5,000m in summer. They are renowned fighting birds, and have a loud, chuckling call.

BLUE-BREASTED QUAIL *C. chinensis.* 13cm. A tiny, shy quail, partial to tall thin grass or reeds, deserted cultivation or crops. It occurs in suitable areas in Peninsular and eastern India, Bangladesh and Sri Lanka. They fly only a short distance when put up, and are difficult to see on the ground – the most likely place being in low grass at the side of a track. The small covies fly fast and low, just skimming the vegetation, and prefer a wetter habitat than most quails.

JUNGLE BUSH-QUAIL *Perdicula asiatica.* 17cm. This handsome little quail is resident throughout most of India and Sri Lanka, except in dry areas of the north-west and Bangladesh. It is almost always to be found in covies which tend to flush explosively under one's feet with the birds scattering in all directions. It is partial to dry grassland or jungle in the plains or foothills.

LITTLE BUSTARD-QUAIL *Turnix sylvatica.* 14cm. This is not a true quail at all, having only three toes. The female is larger, but the male alone tends the eggs and young, and several males are courted by one hen, who makes a curious soft drumming noise to advertise her presence. A bird of grassy places or scrub; occurs in the plains or hills throughout the area except Sri Lanka.

SARUS CRANE *Grus antigone.* 150cm. It is difficult to overlook this impressive and stately bird – nearly as tall as a man – on the jheels and marshes where it lives. It pairs for life, the two birds always staying so close together as to have inspired much folk-lore about their fidelity, and is, by common consent, allowed to live unmolested. It is, in consequence, much less wary than the two migratory cranes. It has a loud trumpeting call, uttered with the neck and bill stretched up, the male often fluffing the back feathers and secondaries up while pressing the primaries stiffly down. One bird of a pair always answers the other's call. In the nuptial display the two birds dance round each other with little jumps and bows, the whole performance lasting several minutes. It is widely distributed across northern India from Pakistan to Assam.

COMMON CRANE *G. grus.* 120cm. Grey cranes found in winter in flocks are likely to be of this or the next species, both being migratory. The sight of a large flock in flight is most impressive, being enhanced by the loud resonant trumpeting calls. Found on flooded meadows or jheels, cranes are constantly on the alert, and feed mostly in the mornings and evenings in crops, where they can do much damage. They visit the plains country of northern India between October and March.

DEMOISELLE CRANE *Anthropoides virgo.* 90cm. Breeds over a smaller area of Eurasia than the Common Crane, but visits India in perhaps even larger numbers. Most common in the north-west, becoming rare in the south and Bangladesh. It prefers rather more arid and stony habitats to the larger bird, although both species may often be found together.

GREAT INDIAN BUSTARD *Choriotis nigriceps.* 120cm. Now becoming rare in the dry, open grasslands of north-west India, it was once common and ranged through Pakistan and Peninsular India. The spread of cultivation is one adverse factor, but it is still shot from vehicles despite the evident need for its preservation, as it occurs nowhere else in the world. It is usually seen in small flocks, but they are very shy and wary, and often prefer to run rather than fly when disturbed. The male has an elaborate display when the neck feathers are fluffed out and an inflatable pouch of skin expanded, the tail is spread and elevated, and the wings drooped, while he pirouettes around an apparently uninterested hen. The male is about a third larger than the female, and weighs up to 14kg.

LIKH *Sypheotides indica.* 50cm. Smallest and least shy of the bustards, it has a wide range through the drier grasslands of Pakistan, northern and central India and the Himalayan foothills. It is not a particularly gregarious bird, and the cocks attract the hens in the breeding season by fluttering up into the air from a low mound or open patch, and making a croaking call. They take no interest in the raising of the brood, and probably mate with several females. The four eggs are laid on the bare ground.

BENGAL FLORICAN *Eupodotis bengalensis.* 63cm. Found in the grassland areas north and east of the Ganges. The cock has a distinctive display flight, watched by several hens, when he jumps into the air and floats slowly down again. He also displays on the ground, strutting round the hen with expanded tail. Although best adapted for running or walking, bustards have large powerful wings, and are strong, steady fliers, holding the neck stretched out. Owing to their good eating qualities, both this bird and the Likh are extensively shot.

HOUBARA *Chlamydotis undulata.* 70cm. A regular visitor in winter to Pakistan and N.W. India, generally found singly or in small groups, which frequent semi-desert, river flood-plains or coastal dunes. Extremely wary and difficult to approach on foot, although they are shot from vehicles to an extent where their status in Pakistan is a matter of great concern. Like other bustards, they are omnivorous, feeding on grain, berries, lizards and snakes.

GREAT INDIAN BUSTARD
♀
♂
LIKH
♂
♀
BENGAL
FLORICAN
♂
HOUBARA
♀
♂

ad
imm
WHITE-BREAST
WATERHEN
RUDDY CRAKE
SLATY-BREASTED RAIL
ad
MOORHEN
imm
COOT

WHITE-BREASTED WATERHEN *Amaurornis phoenicurus.* 30cm. A familiar waterside bird, found throughout the area except in the arid parts of the north-west. Haunts thick cover around the edges of jheels, village ponds or marshes, attracting attention by its medley of raucous creaking and clicking notes. Like some of its relatives, it is a pugnacious bird. Often feeds out in the open on vegetable or insect life, but runs quickly for cover when alarmed. It breeds during the rains, often placing the nest well above water-level.

RUDDY CRAKE *A. fuscus.* 20cm. Living in thick, tangled swamp vegetation, it is a difficult bird to watch, although it may sometimes be seen picking its way over an open patch of mud in the early morning. When alarmed it vanishes immediately in the herbage. Has a repeated metallic note. When flying, the weak fluttery wing-beats and dangling legs are typical of the family. It is found throughout the area.

SLATY-BREASTED RAIL *Rallus striatus.* 28cm. A skulking bird of marshes and waterside vegetation, found in suitable areas through northern and peninsular India to Sri Lanka. It walks daintily across the mud, rather like a miniature chicken, with bobbing head and constantly flirted tail. The long toes and slim body, flattened at the sides, make for easy movement through thick grass and reeds.

MOORHEN *Gallinula chloropus.* 30cm. One of the best known of waterside birds. Like the Coot, it is more addicted to swimming than the rest of the family, and does this with a typical jerking of the head as it paddles. When walking the tail is held up and flirted to show the white patch underneath. Although fairly sociable, it is pugnacious, and has a loud, explosive call which echoes across the water. Found throughout the area on ponds, lakes, jheels or ditches.

COOT *Fulica atra.* 40cm. The most aquatic of the rail family, it has broad, flat lobes along the sides of its toes, and paddles more smoothly and efficiently than a Moorhen. When taking off from the water, it has to patter along before getting airborne properly, but then flies well. Frequents open waters, gathering in large herds in winter in Pakistan and the north-west. It is found throughout the area, the resident population being augmented by winter visitors.

WATERCOCK
♂
♀
PURPLE MOORHEN
BRONZE-WINGED JACANA
PHEASANT-TAILED JACANA

WATERCOCK *Gallicrex cinerea.* 42cm. Resembling an enlarged Moorhen, it is pugnacious in the breeding season, when the male is notable for the fleshy red horn rising from the base of the bill. It is a very skulking bird, spending most of the day in thick water-side vegetation, venturing out at dusk and dawn to feed on crops, seeds or insects. It is noisy, producing a regular series of hollow, strident notes. Found throughout the lowlands, it nests during the rains, building in rushes at the edge of a jheel or wet field.

PURPLE MOORHEN *Porphyrio porphyrio.* 42cm. It is fascinating to see this apparently heavy and clumsy rail clambering about easily in reed-beds, grasping the stems with its long toes. Rarely seen in flight, it spends most of the time lurking in thick, swampy vegetation, often in small parties. It shares the family habit of flicking the tail up to display the white coverts underneath. Found throughout the area south of the Himalayas, but uncommon in Kashmir.

BRONZE-WINGED JACANA *Metopidius indicus.* 27cm. The greatly lengthened toes and claws of Jacanas enable them to walk easily on floating vegetation, and they can therefore exploit a feeding habitat which is intermediate between those of rails and ducks. They can also swim and dive, and submerge the body like a grebe when alarmed. Often on weed-covered ponds by villages or towns, they are not difficult to watch as they move about, feeding on aquatic plant and insect life. Found throughout the peninsular, and in the north and north-east.

PHEASANT-TAILED JACANA *Hydrophasianus chirurgus.* 58cm, with tail. One of the most unusual-looking and elegant of the water-birds, it occurs from the Himalayas southwards, and is common in Sri Lanka. It is very distinctive in flight, when the white, black-edged wings contrast with the dark body. Although quite often seen on the wing, it is not a strong flier, and is a resident species.

PAINTED SNIPE *Rostratula benghalensis.* 25cm. Although resembling the true snipes in plumage, this is in fact a relative of the rails. Like them it flies slowly on rounded wings, the legs dangling loosely. Usually seen singly or in small parties, it is more active at dawn or dusk than in the heat of the day. The female is brighter and rather larger than the male, and apart from laying the eggs has nothing to do with bringing up the family. Found on swamps, jheels or ditches throughout the area, but uncommon in Nepal.

RED-WATTLED LAPWING *Vanellus indicus.* 33cm. A common and familiar bird of cultivation, open country and marshes, it is found throughout the area. Often noisy, it has a loud, ringing four-note call, and is generally to be seen in pairs. The flight is rather slow compared with most plovers, the rounded wings flapping heavily. The four eggs are laid in a natural scrape on the ground or in vegetation.

YELLOW-WATTLED LAPWING *V. malabaricus.* 25cm. This Lapwing has a more restricted range, being confined to northern and peninsular India and Sri Lanka. It prefers drier country, such as stubble fields and waste ground, and is a quieter and less neurotic bird, with a softer double call-note.

LITTLE RINGED PLOVER *Charadrius dubius.* 15cm. Like other plovers, it has the characteristic habit of running along, then stopping suddenly to peck at the ground, tilting the body down almost mechanically. A resident species throughout the area, it frequents dried-up mud-flats, shingly or sandy rivers and tank margins, and the coast. It has a low, quiet note.

KENTISH PLOVER *C. alexandrinus.* 15cm. Breeding in Pakistan, the north-west and Sri Lanka, it is more widely distributed in winter. Often found with other small waders, it is very active, the short legs twinkling as it dashes across the mud. It has a liquid double alarm-call.

GREAT SAND PLOVER *C. leschenaultii.* 21cm. Often in large flocks which feed over the mud-flats and estuaries, it is, with the Lesser Sand-Plover, one of the commonest waders. It is a winter visitor to all coasts. The manoeuvres of a closely packed flock in flight catch the eye as all the birds turn simultaneously, flashing silver in the sun as they show their white underparts.

LESSER GOLDEN PLOVER *Pluvialis dominica.* 25cm. A winter visitor to the coasts and wetter inland areas of southern and eastern India and Sri Lanka; less common in the north and west. Usually in flocks, it is a shy bird, taking wing at the first sign of danger. It migrates huge distances from its breeding grounds in the far north.

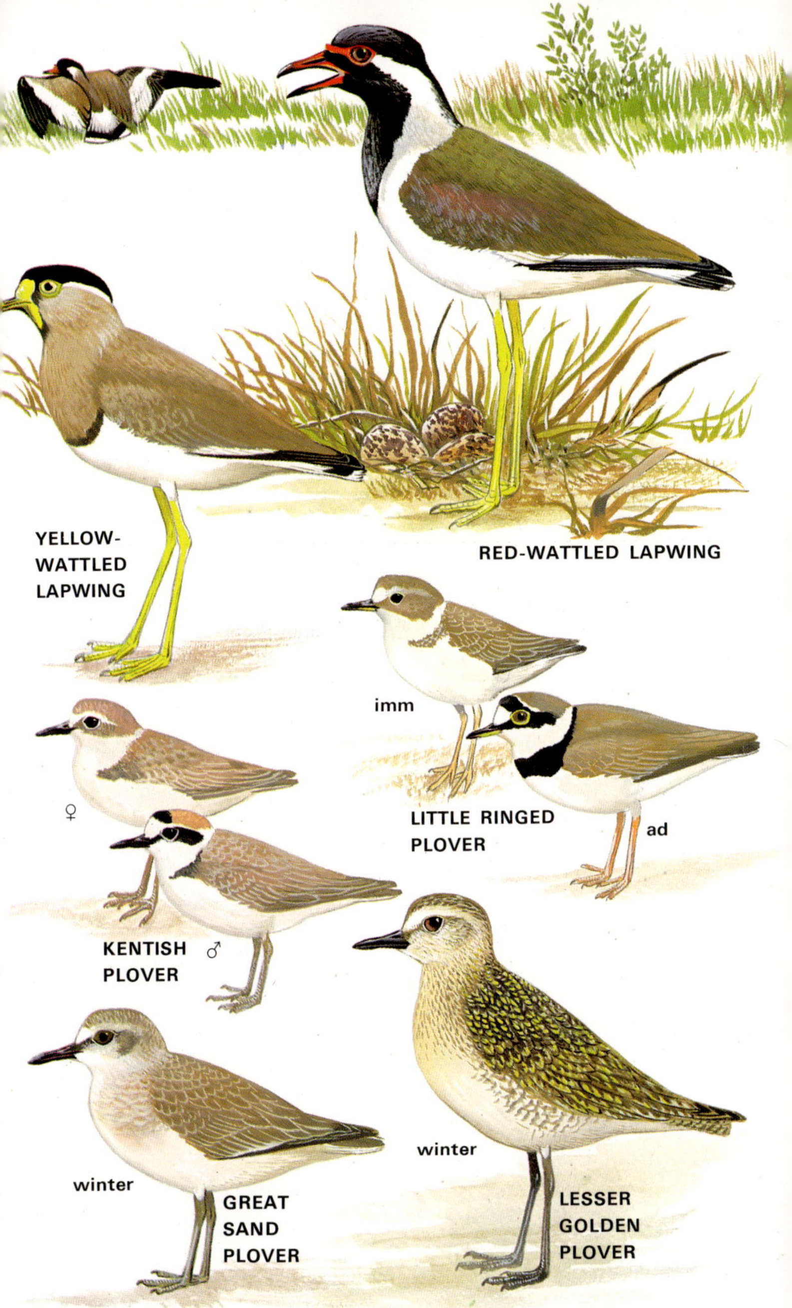
YELLOW-
WATTLED
LAPWING
RED-WATTLED LAPWING
imm
LITTLE RINGED
PLOVER
ad
♀
KENTISH
PLOVER
♂
winter
GREAT
SAND
PLOVER
winter
LESSER
GOLDEN
PLOVER

COMMON SNIPE *Gallinago gallinago.* 24cm. Usually seen as it rockets up from the edge of a ditch, uttering a scratchy note, and turning and twisting in flight. It probes deep in the mud for worms, and the eye is set high on the side of the head so as to give maximum visibility when feeding. Breeding in Kashmir and the Himalayas, it is abundant in winter throughout the area, in wet fields, marshes or ditches.

WOOD SANDPIPER *Tringa glareola.* 23cm. A most characteristic bird of shallow pools, wallows or jheels and pond margins in winter. It does not form close flocks like some of the shore waders, and, not being unduly shy, can be watched as it feeds actively through the water, snapping briskly at bugs and flies.

COMMON SANDPIPER *T. hypoleucos.* 20cm. Breeding by hill streams in the western Himalayas, it is a common winter visitor throughout the rest of the area. Often seen singly on rocky or sandy river banks, creeks, tank margins or the coast, it bobs nervously as it moves about. When it flies out low over the water, the wings look bowed, and are beaten shallowly to give a flickering appearance.

LITTLE STINT *Calidris minutus.* 15cm. This tiny and attractive little bird breeds in the far north, and winters on mudflats, or lagoon or tank margins throughout the area, abundant in north-west India and Sri Lanka. Very active, it is constantly searching for the small aquatic animals on which it feeds. It is a swift flier, forming closely packed flocks in the air, which twist and turn with typical precision.

CURLEW *Numenius arquata.* 58cm. The wild, haunting cry from which it gets its name can be heard at a great distance, and draws attention to the flock flying along the distant shoreline. The long, curved bill is used for probing into the mud for worms and molluscs on which it feeds. It is a very wary bird, often the first to take alarm on the shore, spreading unease through other feeding flocks. Winters on coasts throughout the area.

COMMON SNIPE
WOOD SANDPIPER
COMMON SANDPIPER
summer
winter
LITTLE STINT
CURLEW

BLACK-WINGED STILT *Himantopus himantopus.* 37cm. It is difficult to mistake this elegant and striking shorebird for any other species, and fascinating to watch one wading steadily through the water, snapping delicately at flies and other aquatic insects as it goes, sometimes ducking its head under the surface. A noisy bird; several pairs will band together to mob an intruder with repeated yelping calls. A resident species throughout the area.

STONE CURLEW *Burhinus oedicnemus.* 40cm. Found on dry, open grassland, scrub, or rocky ground with scattered trees. A nocturnal bird for the most part, as is suggested by the large eyes, and certainly noisier at night. When disturbed it prefers running to flying, but if pressed it flaps low over the ground to pitch out of sight behind a rise. When walking the body is held horizontal, the bird stretching up every now and again to look around.

LITTLE PRATINCOLE *Glareola lactea.* 17cm. Often in large flocks about sandbanks and river-beds, where it nests before the rains swell water levels. It spends much time on the wing, wheeling about with agile flight catching insects. It is found throughout the area.

INDIAN COURSER *Cursorius coromandelicus.* 25cm. A bird of dry, open scrub and fallow fields, it is hard to spot when standing still, but its habit of running in brief spurts across open ground soon attracts attention. It bobs down like a small plover to pick up a beetle or other morsel, then stretches up alertly to scan the surroundings. It runs rapidly ahead of an intruder until forced into flight, and is found throughout the area.

CHESTNUT-BELLIED SANDGROUSE *Pterocles exustus.* 29cm. Frequents similar country to the Courser, being even more addicted to wide, barren sandy areas. Apart from Sri Lanka, N.E. India and Bangladesh, it is found throughout the area. Usually in small parties, but large numbers gather to drink in the early morning. Often fly long distances to water, are fast and agile on the wing, but waddl awkwardly on the ground.

♀
♂ breeding
BLACK-WINGED
STILT
LITTLE
PRATINCOLE
ad
imm
INDIAN COURSER
STONE CURLEW
♀
♂
CHESTNUT-BELLIED
SANDGROUSE

1st winter
ad winter
ad breeding
BLACK-HEADED GULL
ad winter
ad breeding
BROWN-HEADED GULL
breeding
winter
RIVER TERN
winter
WHISKERE
TERN
winter
BLACK-BELLIED
TERN
summer
summer

BLACK-HEADED GULL *Larus ridibundus.* 40cm. A winter visitor to sea-coasts and inland lakes and rivers. It is particularly common in Pakistan and N.W. India, but is not yet recorded from Sri Lanka. A familiar bird around harbours and fishing villages, it scavenges from the beaches or tideline, and is constantly to be seen wheeling around or beating steadily over the water in search of something edible. Best distinguished from the next species by the wing pattern.

BROWN-HEADED GULL *L. brunnicephalus.* 44cm. Found in winter on all coasts, although never far out to sea, and also on some inland waters. An effortless flier, turning the head this way and that as it floats along, always ready to lower its legs and plunge down to the water and join the scrimmage for a dead fish or other morsel. Both species acquire the dark heads of summer plumage in early spring, before migrating north.

INDIAN RIVER TERN *Sterna aurantia.* 40cm. A river-haunting tern, it occurs in the plains throughout Pakistan, India and Bangladesh. Although not especially sociable, several may beat up and down over the same stretch of water, now and again plunging in head-first to re-appear, if lucky, with a little glistening fish. Nests on sand-bars or islands, and, like other terns, noisily attacks intruders.

BLACK-BELLIED TERN *S. acuticauda.* 33cm. Often consorts with the previous species, but is slighter and more agile, and catches insects in the air as well as plunging for fish. It is found on lakes or rivers throughout the area, although absent from Sri Lanka.

WHISKERED TERN *Chlidonias hybrida.* 25cm. An insect eater, this is a gregarious tern and is usually to be seen hawking gracefully over flooded fields, ponds or jheels, dipping down now and then to ruffle the surface. It breeds across north India from Kashmir to Assam, and is found throughout the area in winter.

GREEN PIGEON *Treron phoenicoptera.* 33cm. Although brightly coloured, green pigeons are not easy to spot high up in a leafy tree, and it is often surprising to see how many can be disturbed from the branches. They burst out with a typical clatter of wings, and have a fast, direct flight. A stout and heavy bird, it is a voracious fruit-eater, and rarely visits the ground. The soles of the feet are swollen and fleshy to assist in grasping the twigs and branches. It is widely distributed throughout the area in woodlands, gardens or avenues.

COLLARED DOVE *Streptopelia decaocto.* 30cm. Very common and familiar throughout the area except in the eastern Himalayas, its sleepy cooing can be heard in all gardens, cultivated areas and light woodland. A gregarious bird, gathering in flocks to feed on the stubbles, and flying up with strong, noisy wing-beats.

LITTLE BROWN DOVE *S. senegalensis.* 25cm. Tame, and perhaps even more familiar than the Collared Dove, since it constantly frequents paths, verandahs and roofs. A bird of dry woodland and cultivation, avoiding heavy forests, it occurs through Pakistan and northern and Peninsular India, but is absent from Assam and Sri Lanka.

SPOTTED DOVE *S. chinensis.* 30cm. Very widely distributed in southern Asia, it is found throughout our area, frequenting rather lush wooded countryside. It is a popular cagebird, and is familiar around villages and gardens, where it walks about on the paths picking up grain. It has a longer series of cooing phrases than the Collared Dove.

RED TURTLE DOVE *S. tranquebarica.* 22cm. This little dove often looks quite a brilliant red as it flies up into a leafy tree in strong sunlight. Not such a confiding bird as some of its relatives, and markedly less partial to the neighbourhood of man. It is very widely distributed, although rare in Sri Lanka, and avoids only heavy forest or desert.

BLUE ROCK PIGEON *Columba livia.* 32cm. Abundant around cities and towns throughout the area, there are still wild populations of this pigeon, which live around ruins or cliffs, feeding in nearby fields. The rich throaty coo, and strutting, neck-swelling display of the cock are well known to all.

COLLARED
DOVE
imm
ad
LITTLE
BROWN
DOVE
SPOTTED
DOVE
RED
TURTLE DOVE
BLUE ROCK PIGEON

INDIAN LORIKEET *Loriculus vernalis.* 15cm. These little birds are difficult to see as they clamber about the branches of a fruiting or flowering tree, although the squeaky triple whistle is, when learnt, a sure guide to their presence. They are sociable birds, gathering in small flocks to feed in a suitably attractive tree, following one another with quick, dipping flight across the clearings. They have the curious habit of roosting upside-down, hanging from a branch by the feet. They are found in the Himalayas from Nepal eastwards, and in W. and E. Peninsular India through to Assam, in forests or woodland in the plains and foothills. A related species lives in Sri Lanka.

ROSE-RINGED PARAKEET *Psittacula krameri.* 40cm. The most abundant and well-known of its family, this parakeet is to be found throughout the area in light woodland, parks, gardens and cultivated areas. It is a pest of some importance, as the noisy flocks do much damage to crops and fruit. Although beautifully adapted for climbing about in trees, with two toes pointing forwards and two behind, they sometimes visit the ground, sidling about with a rolling gait on their short legs. The nest is placed in a hole in a tree, those with small entrances being suitably enlarged, or sometimes in cracks or holes in masonry. These and other parakeets are favourite cagebirds, but are not especially good at learning to speak.

ALEXANDRINE PARAKEET *P. eupatria.* 50cm. A voracious bird, capable of doing great damage to crops, flowers or fruit with its powerful beak. Very sociable and noisy, it sometimes gathers in large flocks at roosts, often with other species. The nest is placed in a hole high in a tree, only rarely near human habitation. This parakeet is very widely distributed in wooded country.

BLOSSOM-HEADED PARAKEET *P. cyanocephala.* 37cm. Less well known than the other species shown, it is not often kept as a pet, and does not so often frequent trees and avenues round towns and villages. It is more a bird of forests and cultivated areas in wooded country, and is widely distributed. It has a more musical call than the harsh screeching of the other parakeets, and is if anything even more arboreal; it also has a particularly swift flight.

♂
ROSE-RINGED PARAKEET
♀
♀
♂
ALEXANDRINE PARAKEET
♀
♂
BLOSSOM-HEADED PARAKEET

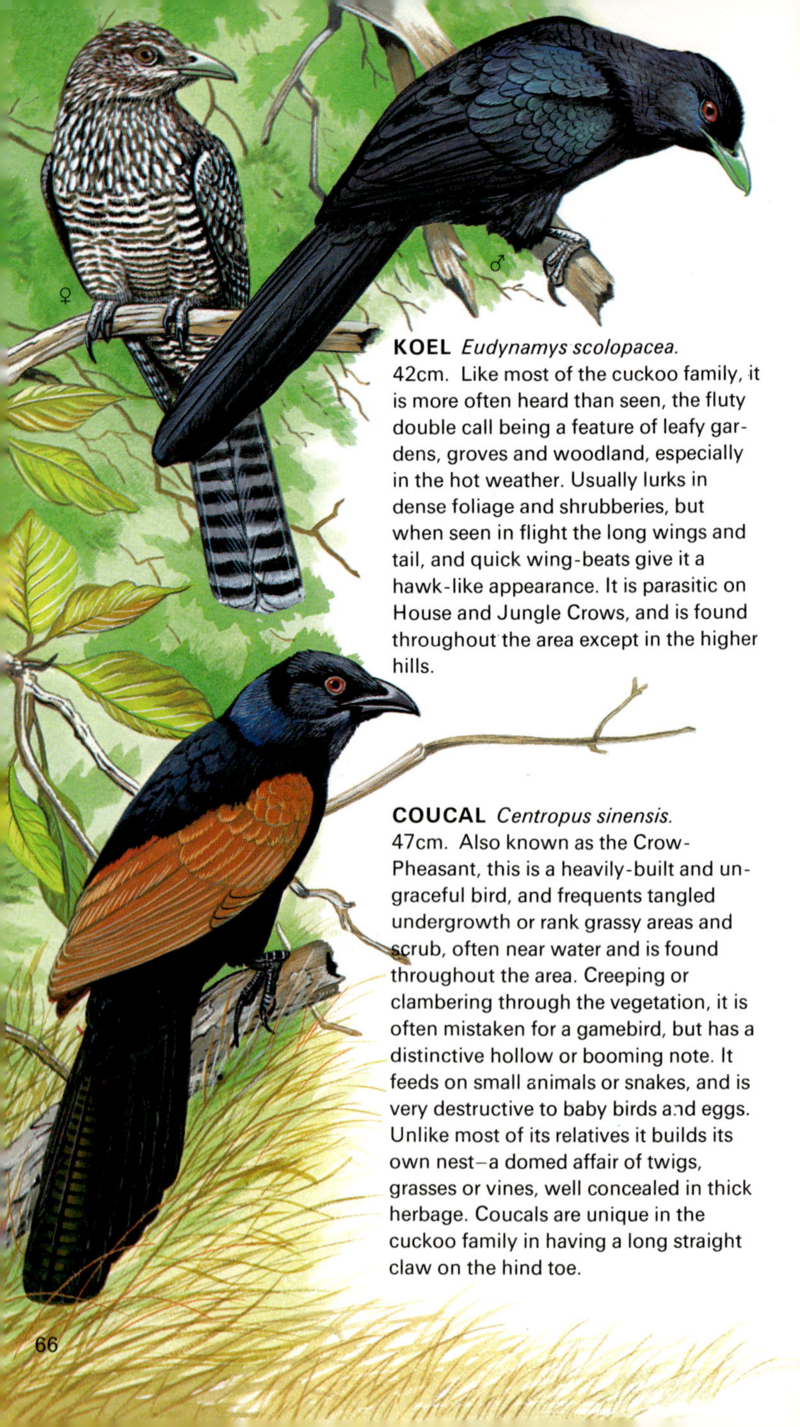

KOEL *Eudynamys scolopacea.*
42cm. Like most of the cuckoo family, it is more often heard than seen, the fluty double call being a feature of leafy gardens, groves and woodland, especially in the hot weather. Usually lurks in dense foliage and shrubberies, but when seen in flight the long wings and tail, and quick wing-beats give it a hawk-like appearance. It is parasitic on House and Jungle Crows, and is found throughout the area except in the higher hills.

COUCAL *Centropus sinensis.*
47cm. Also known as the Crow-Pheasant, this is a heavily-built and ungraceful bird, and frequents tangled undergrowth or rank grassy areas and scrub, often near water and is found throughout the area. Creeping or clambering through the vegetation, it is often mistaken for a gamebird, but has a distinctive hollow or booming note. It feeds on small animals or snakes, and is very destructive to baby birds and eggs. Unlike most of its relatives it builds its own nest—a domed affair of twigs, grasses or vines, well concealed in thick herbage. Coucals are unique in the cuckoo family in having a long straight claw on the hind toe.

PIED CRESTED CUCKOO *Clamator jacobinus.* 33cm. Resident in Sri Lanka and the south of the Peninsular, it is a summer visitor to the north and west. It occurs in most types of wooded countryside in the lowlands, and is parasitic on babblers, though much remains to be learnt of its breeding biology and its seasonal movements. It is noisy, having a loud disyllabic note, and is somewhat easier to see than most cuckoos, being less confined to the forest canopy, and less shy.

BRAINFEVER BIRD *Cuculus varius.* 33cm. The endlessly repeated triple call, becoming more frenzied as it rises higher and higher, gives this common cuckoo its unflattering name. It is also known as the Hawk-Cuckoo. Rarely seen, it keeps to tall trees in wooded countryside, and could certainly be mistaken for a hawk at a quick glance. It is parasitic, and, considerately, becomes silent after the breeding season. It is found throughout the plains, except in the arid northwest, but it is less common in Sri Lanka.

Δ

INDIAN PLAINTIVE CUCKOO *Cacomantis merulinus.* 22cm. Better known for its voice than its appearance, it has a loud double or triple whistle. Found in wooded countryside, bushy gardens and thickets throughout the area except in arid parts of the north-west. It lays its eggs in the nests of various warblers, and ceases calling after the breeding season, becoming unobtrusive and hard to locate.

INDIAN EAGLE-OWL
BROWN FISH-OWL

INDIAN EAGLE-OWL *Bubo bubo.* 60cm. A powerful and impressive bird, frequenting rocky, broken country with ravines, scrub, groves and light woodland. Not in Sri Lanka, but widespread elsewhere, being more common in the north. It may sometimes be seen in day-time, when, it is liable to be mobbed by other birds. Best known for its deep, sonorous double hoot.

BROWN FISH-OWL *Ketupa zeylonensis.* 55cm. Superficially similar to the Eagle-Owl, it has bare legs and feet adapted for catching and holding the fish on which it lives. Frequents river-valleys, streams, pools and backwaters, roosting in a large tree or cliff-face by day, and venturing out to feed at dusk. It has a deep booming call, and nests on a rocky ledge or in a hole in a tree. It is widely distributed, except in the higher hills.

SPOTTED OWLET *Athene brama.* 20cm. One of the most familiar owls, it is often seen around buildings or in old hollow trees in gardens or villages. When disturbed at its roost, it glares at the intruder, bobbing and ducking comically, then flies off with typically bounding action on rounded wings. It is found throughout the area except in Sri Lanka, but avoids thick forest.

JUNGLE OWLET *Glaucidium radiatum.* 20cm. More of a thick woodland and jungle dweller than the Spotted Owlet, it occurs from the Himalayas south to Sri Lanka, though not in the north-west.

COLLARED SCOPS OWL *Otus bakkamoena.* 25cm. A very widely distributed and variable owl. Almost totally nocturnal; very difficult to see in daytime, even when in full view on a branch. It makes a familiar soft, single note at regular intervals. It is widespread in forests, orchards and gardens, in plains or hills.

△ **INDIAN NIGHTJAR** *Caprimulgus asiaticus.* 25cm. Usually seen at dusk flitting over a garden or forest glade. Nightjars feed on moths, and have a beautifully controlled but apparently aimless and erratic flight. Often sitting on roads or tracks, their eyes gleam red as they reflect a car's headlights. The call is distinctive – several hard notes running into a short, dry churr. Found throughout the area in open, bushy or lightly wooded country.

PALM SWIFT *Cypsiurus parvus.* 13cm. Widespread except in Pakistan, but confined to localities with palm-trees. Several pairs nests in the same tree, and spend much time swooping around nearby. The breeding season seems to last all year, the tiny, purse-shaped nest being glued to the underside of a palm leaf.

CRESTED TREE SWIFT *Hemiprocne longipennis.* 22cm. The crest gives this bird a distinctive silhouette as it perches upright on a bare branch. It has a rather un-swift-like flight, wheeling rather slowly and gracefully about. The nest is like a tiny saucer stuck on a branch, almost invisible from below. It frequents forests, especially clearings and glades, throughout the area, except in Pakistan.

ALPINE SWIFT *Apus melba.* 22cm. Locally resident in India and Sri Lanka, it is liable to be seen anywhere owing to its powers of flight. Information is lacking on many possible breeding sites, which are usually on inaccessible cliffs. The speed with which a screaming party will swoop down a hillside and wheel out over the valley is thrilling, and as night falls they spiral higher and higher until lost to view.

HOUSE SWIFT *A. affinis.* 15cm. A very gregarious and familiar species, breeding in colonies in towns, forts, bridges and similar places. The birds fly around in swirling flocks which often ascend high in the air, and make a shrill chittering noise. Breeding is carried on sporadically through the year. A widely distributed species.

PALM SWIFT
TREE SWIFT
ALPINE SWIFT
HOUSE SWIFT

WHITE-BREASTED KINGFISHER
Halcyon smyrnensis. 27cm. Found throughout the area, this conspicuous bird of open forest, marshes, cultivation or gardens feeds on frogs, lizards, beetles or other small animals, and watches for these from a perch on a post or dead tree. Its loud, cackling scream is often uttered from a tree-top. Nest is a hole in a dry earth bank.

PIED KINGFISHER *Ceryle rudis.* 30cm. Common by canals, lakes or ponds throughout the plains. A specialist at fishing from the air, it may even be seen hovering over water in busy towns, tail depressed and heavy bill pointing straight down. When perched on a waterside stump or pole it flicks its tail up and down.

◁ **COMMON KINGFISHER** *Alcedo atthis.* 18cm. Perhaps less shy than its larger relatives, this kingfisher is found throughout the area. It is often to be seen perched on a stick or branch overlooking a ditch or pool, watching intently for fish. It nests in a tunnel by the waterside.

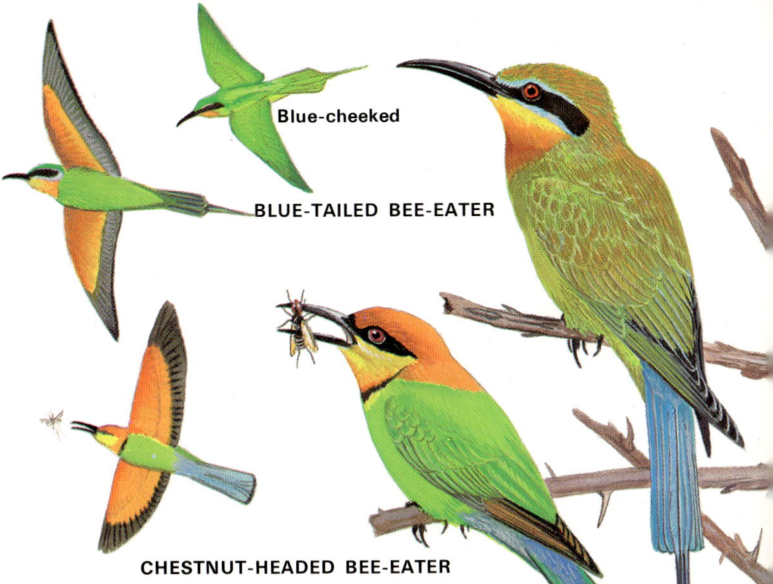

CHESTNUT-HEADED BEE-EATER

Merops leschenaulti. 22cm. One of the most attractive birds of open country, it is typically to be seen is small flocks, often perched in a leafless tree from which individuals glide out now and again to pursue a flying insect. It occurs in the Himalayan foothills, N.E. India and Bangladesh, the W. Ghats and Sri Lanka.

BLUE-TAILED BEE-EATER *M. philippinus.* 30cm. Breeding widely except in Sri Lanka and S. Peninsular India. Bee-Eaters catch in flight such fast and agile insects as dragonflies, although the usual diet is bees, and nest in holes in sandy banks or soft ground.

LITTLE GREEN BEE-EATER *M. orientalis.* 22cm. Common in open or lightly wooded countryside, deserts or cultivation. Often seen perched on posts, where the birds line up side by side, constantly changing places as first one, then another, launches out after an insect. ▷

GREAT PIED
HORNBILL
GREY
HORNBILL
HOOPOE

GREAT PIED HORNBILL *Buceros bicornis.* 125cm. This splendid hornbill occurs in small parties in forests in the Himalayan foothills, N.E., and S.W. India, but is declining in numbers as a result of de-forestation and shooting. In flight, the wings make a loud droning sound – often the only indication of the bird as it flies over tree-tops in heavy forest, and it also has a loud, deep cackling note. It is shy, and keeps much to the trees, only rarely descending to the ground, and feeds largely on fruit.

COMMON GREY HORNBILL *Tockus birostris.* 65cm. Found widely across north India and the Himalayan foothills to Peninsular India, but not in Bangladesh, S.W. India, or Sri Lanka. It keeps to large trees in woodland, avenues or cultivated areas, going about in small parties, and in flight flaps heavily, with short gliding periods. Like other hornbills, it nests in a hole in a tree, in which the female imprisons herself during incubation by plastering up the entrance. She is fed by the male through a slit left for the purpose.

HOOPOE *Upupa epops.* 30cm. As it feeds on the ground – often around houses or on cultivated areas – and is tame, it is a familiar bird. The long, curved bill is used for probing in dung-heaps or in the turf for beetles and grubs; the crest is usually only erected when the bird is uneasy, or on alighting. It takes its name from the distinctive hollow, hooting call, and is widely distributed in open or cultivated country.

INDIAN ROLLER *Coracias benghalensis.* 30cm. Also known as the Blue Jay – a name which becomes most appropriate when the bird flaps down to the grass from a telegraph wire, showing the brilliant turquoise and blue pattern on the wings. It feeds on beetles and other insects caught on the ground, and when on the look-out for these, perched on a post or tree, appears a rather dull and lumpy bird. It occurs throughout the area. It is replaced in Kashmir by a closely-related species.

COPPERSMITH *Megalaima haemacephala.* 15cm. The metallic, single note of this small barbet is a familiar and monotonous call in the plains throughout the area, wherever there are trees. Although closely related to woodpeckers, the barbets have not developed a stiff tail for support while climbing, and spend much time sitting in the leafy tops of trees, or searching for fruit.

GREEN BARBET *M. zeylanica.* 25cm. Very common throughout the lowlands, its loud two-note call echoes across the countryside. It is found in all well-timbered areas, gardens or avenues in towns, and like other barbets hacks its nest-hole out of a tree, often in decaying wood. The bill is an even more powerful chisel than that of a woodpecker; the reason for the bristles around the base is not yet known.

BLUE-THROATED BARBET *M. asiatica.* 22cm. A common bird of wooded country in the Himalayas, N.E. India and Bangladesh It has a distinctive rolling three-note call, very familiar around hill villages, although the bird itself often remains concealed near the top of a tree. While individual birds constantly reply to each other's calls, barbets seem to be rather solitary, except when gathering at a fruiting tree, when they have to share the feast with several other species.

MAHRATTA WOODPECKER *Dendrocopos mahrattensis.* 17 cm. A common woodpecker, found throughout the area except in the extreme north-west and the north-east. It occurs in light woodland, gardens, or in lines of trees by paths or roads. The speckled plumage is protective as it moves quietly around the trunk of a shade-dappled tree, but it often attracts attention by drumming loudly on dead wood. It bores a small, neat nest-hole, often quite low down on a tree-trunk or branch.

GOLDEN-BACKED WOODPECKER *Dinopium benghalense.* 27cm. Perhaps the commonest of the woodpeckers, it occurs throughout the area including Sri Lanka, although here the local race has a scarlet rather than gold back. Not unduly shy, it may be watched as it hitches up a tree-trunk, tapping here and there for grubs, or calling with a loud cackle to its mate a few trees away. Sometimes flies down to the ground to rummage about for ants, on which it often feeds. Found in most types of wooded country.

◁ **INDIAN PITTA** *Pitta brachyura.* 18cm. One of the most beautiful birds in India, it lives in forest or scrub, spending most of the time on the ground. It is migratory, wintering in Peninsular India and Sri Lanka, and breeding in northern India to the Himalayan foothills and Assam. Pittas have a clear double whistle which often draws attention to their presence, but are not especially shy, and can readily be watched hopping about in gardens where there is plenty of cover. They make a domed nest of twigs and grass, placed low down in a bush or tree-fork.

ASHY-CROWNED FINCH-LARK *Eremopterix grisea.* 13cm. A common bird, it is usually seen on dusty open ground or fallow fields, and occurs throughout the area in the plains and foothills. In the display flight, the male sings his trilling song while circling over the nesting area, rising and falling in steep undulations. On the ground, the birds creep about unobtrusively with legs well flexed as they search for seeds.

RED-WINGED BUSH-LARK *Mirafra erythroptera.* 14cm. With the exception of Bangladesh, Sri Lanka and Kerala, this lark is resident everywhere on dry, open or scrub-dotted plains. In the song-flight, it flutters up vertically, parachuting down again with wings raised.

CRESTED LARK *Galerida cristata.* 18cm. The perky crest and pale coloration mark this large lark, which is found across northern and central India and Pakistan. A resident bird of dry or sandy open country in the plains, it is fond of sitting on telegraph wires, where it utters its short song, and also sings in a circling songflight, often low over the ground.

SMALL SKYLARK *Alauda gulgula.* 17cm. Noteworthy for its sustained and lively chirruping song, delivered as it flutters up vertically from the ground, the performance being the most accomplished of all the larks. Like its relatives, it feeds on seeds, grain and insects, and builds a well-concealed nest on the ground. It is resident throughout the area in open country and grassland.

SHORT-TOED LARK *Calandrella cinerea.* 15cm. A winter visitor to India, often occurring in large flocks on dry open or waste ground, or semi-desert. When disturbed, the birds fly up in a dense drifting cloud, uttering a short call-note, and wheel around before settling further away. They do not perch on bushes or telephone wires.

♀
♂
ASHY-CROWNED FINCH-LARK
RED-WINGED BUSH-LARK
SMALL SKYLARK
CRESTED LARK
SHORT-TOED LARK

WIRE-TAILED SWALLOW
RED-RUMPED SWALLOW
COMMON SWALLOW

DUSKY CRAG MARTIN *Hirundo concolor.* 13cm. Resident in northern and peninsular India, it is less sociable than the migratory swallows. Haunts the vicinity of ruins, cliffs or even constantly used buildings, wheeling about with graceful flight, or perching, almost invisible, on a ledge or rock-face. The nest is a mud saucer, cemented to the surface of a cliff-face or wall.

CLIFF SWALLOW *H. fluvicola.* 12cm. Notably gregarious, and often found in the vicinity of water, it nests in large and obvious colonies. Common in parts of northern, central and peninsular India. Hawks for flies or other insects over rivers or lakes, often in company with other swallows and martins.

WIRE-TAILED SWALLOW *H. smithii.* 21cm. Often found by rivers or other water throughout the plains, but rare in Sri Lanka. The thin tail streamers are not noticeable in flight, but the underparts flash silvery white as the bird banks. Not a markedly sociable bird, it does not nest in colonies, though a favourite bridge may hold several pairs.

RED-RUMPED SWALLOW *H. daurica.* 15cm. Common throughout the area both as a breeding bird and a winter visitor. Looks stockier and is slower on the wing than the Common Swallow, hawking rather deliberately over grass or along a water-course.

COMMON SWALLOW *H. rustica.* 17cm. Breeds in the Himalayas and Assam, dispersing in winter in huge flocks across India to Sri Lanka. Winter flocks often form huge roosts in reedbeds or along power-lines, feeding by day over nearby fields or marshes. Not shy, it often nests in buildings.

Races of Wagtails – males in summer

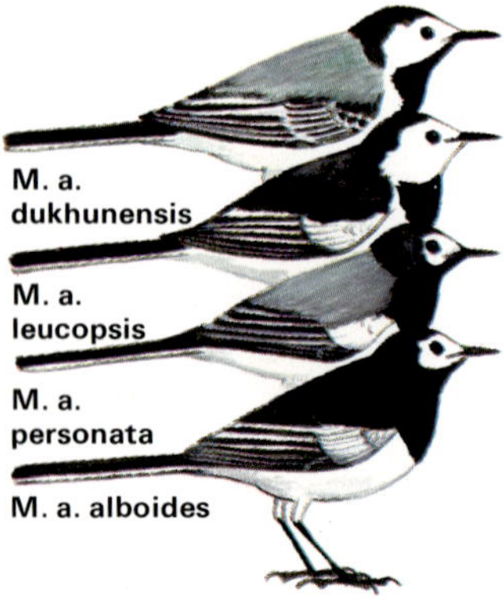

M. a. dukhunensis

M. a. leucopsis

M. a. personata

M. a. alboides

M. f. beema

M. f. thunbergi

M. f. melanogrisea

M. c. citreola

M. c. calcarata

INDIAN PIPIT *Anthus novaeseelandiae.* 15cm. Common throughout the area, on short grass, cultivated or fallow land. Generally in pairs or small parties, it runs quickly over the grass to snap at a small moth or beetle, then stretches upright to survey the surroundings. Has a thin, double call-note.

WHITE WAGTAIL *Motacilla alba.* 17cm. Breeding in the Himalayas, and a common winter visitor south to Sri Lanka. A bird of damp, grassy places or pond-edges, it runs nimbly about after flies, wagging its tail. Several races occur in winter, but are best told as they come into summer plumage. Often seen singly, wagtails are sociable when migrating or roosting, when large numbers gather in crops or reedbeds.

LARGE PIED WAGTAIL *M. maderaspatensis.* 21cm. Resident throughout the area in well-watered countryside; absent in Sri Lanka. It is more partial to the actual waterside – by a pond or stream – than other wagtails, which are content with marshy fields. Nests in a crevice or a hole by a riverbank or bridge.

YELLOW WAGTAIL *M. flava.* 16cm. Even more confusing than the White Wagtail group are the different races of this pretty wagtail when in summer plumage. A winter visitor throughout the area, it is especially fond of wet grassy places or lush fields where cattle disturb the insect-life from underfoot. Like all wagtails, it has a bounding flight, usually not high up, and a rather thin, penetrating double call. Roosts are often large, in a favourite reedbed or patch of rushes, the birds flighting in from the surrounding fields at dusk.

YELLOW-HEADED WAGTAIL *M. citreola.* 16cm. A breeding bird in the Himalayas, wintering southward throughout the area. Often seen in company with other wagtails, it has similar calls and habits, but is perhaps a little less active than the sprightly Yellow Wagtail.

INDIAN
PIPIT
winter
WHITE WAGTAIL
LARGE
PIED WAGTAIL
winter
YELLOW WAGTAIL
winter
YELLOW-HEADED
WAGTAIL

LARGE CUCKOO-SHRIKE
Coracina. novaehollandiae.
28cm. A slow moving and rather unobtrusive bird as it searches through the foliage for caterpillars and other insects. Owes its misleading name to the grey plumage and hooked bill. It has a shrill, screaming call which often draws attention to two or three birds moving through the trees. Widely distributed in woodland throughout the area except in Pakistan and N.W. India.

BLACKHEADED CUCKOO-SHRIKE *C. melanoptera.*
20cm. An inconspicuous bird outside the breeding season, when it is noisy. Although not specially sociable, small parties are sometimes seen searching slowly through the branches, often with other species. It is found in woods, village groves or avenues, in Peninsular India south to Sri Lanka, and in N.E. India and Bangladesh.

COMMON WOOD-SHRIKE *Tephrodornis pondicerianus.* 15cm. Common in the lowlands throughout the area, in light jungle, wooded country or gardens and groves. It is unobtrusive and quiet, but not particularly shy, and can be watched as it gleans the foliage for caterpillars or beetles. Outside the breeding season it occurs in small parties, often in company with other species roving through the woods.

SMALL MINIVET *Pericrocotus cinnamomeus.* 15cm. Attractive and sprightly, it is perhaps more familiar than most of the minivets as it is found in drier and more open country with scattered trees and shrubs, or in scrub and cultivation. It occurs in the plains throughout the area except in parts of Pakistan. Often in parties which flutter actively through the trees, now and again flying out after a passing insect.

SCARLET MINIVET *P. flammeus.* 22cm. It is difficult to imagine a more entrancing sight than a party of these birds flitting through the tree-tops, the patches of red, yellow and black flashing against the green foliage. They frequently utter an attractive whistling note. Breeds in hill forests in the Himalayas, N.E., W., and S. Peninsular India, Sri Lanka and N.E. India.

RED-VENTED BULBUL
RED-WHISKERED BULBUL
P. l. leucoti
WHITE-CHEE
BULBUL
P. l. leucogen
BLACK BULBUL
WHITE-BROWE
BULBUL

RED-VENTED BULBUL *Pycnonotus cafer*. 20cm. One of the most familiar of Indian birds, it abounds in gardens, towns, cultivated country, and scrub throughout the plains and hills up to about 1700m. Bulbuls are mainly arboreal birds, and search through the twigs and foliage for beetles, grubs or fruit, sometimes imitating a flycatcher as they swoop out over the grass after an insect. They have melodious and attractive call-notes, and a short whistling song of several phrases. The Redvented Bulbul is a wary bird, and one of the first to give warning cries on the appearance of a predator. It is a pugnacious bird, and is still trained as a contestant in organised bulbul fights, although also often kept as a pet.

RED-WHISKERED BULBUL *P. jocosus*. 20cm. Absent from Sri Lanka, and most of North-West India and Pakistan, except around Udaipur, but where it does occur it is a very familiar and abundant species. It frequents scrub, woodland and cultivation or gardens around villages, and has an even more pleasant and varied vocabulary than most of its relatives. It likes to sing in full view on the top of a bush, then flies off to the next song-post with a strong but rather uneven flight. It is a confiding bird, and is often kept as a pet.

WHITE-CHEEKED BULBUL *P. leucogenys*. 20cm. A familiar bird in the Himalayas, it also ranges over most of Pakistan and North-West India, where the race occurring in the plains *P. l. leucotis* lacks the jaunty crest. It is found in light woodland, gardens, and the neighbourhood of towns and villages, scrub and mangroves. It is a lively bird, vocal and inquisitive, and places its nest of grasses and roots low down in a hedge or bush, where it is often easy to find. Hybridisation sometimes occurs in the wild between this and the Red-vented Bulbul.

WHITE-BROWED BULBUL *P. luteolus*. 20cm. The quiet, undistinctive plumage suits the more retiring character of this bird, which is common although unobtrusive throughout Peninsular India south to Sri Lanka. It is most easily located by its noisy burst of mellow whistled notes from the thick hedge or clump of bushes where it is hiding. It is partial to gardens, shrubberies and thick cover around villages and towns, and is strictly a bird of the plains.

BLACK BULBUL *Hypsipetes madagascariensis*. 22cm. The Himalayas, and the hills of western and southern India and Sri Lanka are the home of this gregarious and noisy bulbul. It is a bird of the forest canopy, but is easily noticed, as the birds move in a party from one treetop to another with much scratchy calling and commotion. It is often to be seen in company with the mixed hunting parties which are characteristic of hill forests, and feeds on berries and fruit, as well as taking nectar and insects from flowering trees.

GOLD-FRONTED
LEAFBIRD
♀
♂
JERDON'S LEAFBIRD
♀
♂
FAIRY BLUEBIRD

COMMON IORA

COMMON IORA *Aegithina tiphia*. 14cm. This is often a difficult bird to see as it searches unobtrusively through thick foliage for insects. However, it has a well-known descending whistle which betrays its presence in a grove or garden. It is found throughout the area except in much of the north-west in light woodland, scrub, cultivation and gardens in the plains and foothills. It is often to be seen in pairs, and the male has a noteworthy display in which he puffs out his feathers, and prances round the female looking like a brightly coloured ball. The species is unusual among Leafbirds in feeding largely on insects.

GOLD-FRONTED LEAFBIRD *Chloropsis aurifrons.* 19cm. Many of the Leafbirds, which are endemic to southern Asia, are well-known cagebirds, and are often called Fruitsuckers. They feed mainly on nectar, and are consequently often to be seen at such attractive blossoms as those of the Flame of the Forest and Red Silk Cotton trees. They perform a useful service in pollinating flowering trees and shrubs. Like its relatives, this is an active and noisy bird, and is an excellent mimic. Found in wooded country in the plains and foothills bordering the Himalayas to N.E. India, and in the eastern and western peninsular, and Sri Lanka.

JERDON'S LEAFBIRD *C. cochinchinensis.* 18cm. An aggressive bird, it is intolerant of other species feeding in the same tree, and is inclined to hustle them away. It is much given to mimicking other birds, but also has a wide vocabulary of its own. Very acrobatic, it is almost tit-like in its actions as it swings and searches through the blossoms in a tree. It is found in open woodland, gardens or scrub in the plains or hills of peninsular and north-east India and Sri Lanka.

FAIRY BLUEBIRD *Irena puella.* 27cm. To find this beautiful bird one must visit damp hill-forests in the south-west, or the Himalayan foothills or the north-east. It is an arboreal bird, the little parties making a liquid whistling call as they move among the branches. The cock's lovely iridescent plumage is best seen as he flies through the bright shafts of sunlight in a forest glade.

Δ

ASHY SWALLOW-SHRIKE *Artamus fuscus.* 19cm. Despite its name, this is neither a swallow nor a shrike. It occurs throughout the area except in Pakistan, in thin forest or light wooded country with tall trees or palms, and is often to be seen in small groups perched along dead or exposed branches. Every now and then, a bird will swoop out after a passing insect, or wheel around gracefully in a distinctive sailing flight on stiffly-held, triangular wings.

RUFOUS-BACKED SHRIKE *Lanius schach.* 25cm. Shrikes are easily recognised by their habit of keeping a watch-out from the top of a bush or post, from which they glide down to the grass to pounce on an insect or lizard. Adept at keeping their balance on a swaying twig, they swing the tail sideways with a mechanical action. This species occurs throughout the area in several races, one being the black-headed form breeding in the central and eastern Himalayas and wintering in the north-east.

BAY-BACKED SHRIKE *L. vittatus.* 17cm. Frequenting open or cultivated country, it is often to be found in the same small area day after day. It has a low, direct flight with a typical swoop-up to its perch, and is found throughout the area except in the north-east, and Sri Lanka.

BROWN SHRIKE *L. cristatus.* 18cm. A common winter visitor, except to Pakistan and north-west India. Rather shy, it has a raucous chattering note and, like other shrikes, impales its small animal or insect prey on thorns. Often found in thickly forested country, especially in the hills, where it haunts tracksides, glades and clearings.

INDIAN GREY SHRIKE *L. excubitor.* 25cm. Widespread in dry, open countryside, with scattered trees or shrubs, except in the south and Sri Lanka. Although a conspicuous sight as it perches on top of a large, isolated bush it is wary, and does not permit a close approach.

Black-headed race
RUFOUS-BACKED
SHRIKE
BAY-BACKED
SHRIKE
INDIAN GREY
SHRIKE
BROWN SHRIKE

PARADISE FLYCATCHER
◁ ▽ *Terpsiphone paradisi.* 20cm +. Widely distributed except in the north-west. Frequents woodland clearings, gardens or forested ravines, especially near water.

GREY-HEADED FLYCATCHER *Culicicapa ceylonensis.* 12cm. Abundant and widespread in woodland, breeding in the hills.

RED-BREASTED FLYCATCHER
Ficedula parva. 13cm. A common winter visitor to orchards, light woodland or gardens throughout the area.

TICKELL'S FLYCATCHER
Cyornis tickelliae.
14cm. Frequents shady forest or scrub in broken or hilly country throughout the area except the north-west. There are several similar species.

WHITE-BROWED FANTAIL
Rhipidura aureola. 16cm. Fantails are a delight to watch as they flit and posture restlessly in the undergrowth, flirting the tail, and chasing flies, or pirouetting up a tree trunk. Widespread in scrub and woodland.

WHITE-SPOTTED FANTAIL *R. albicollis.* 16cm. Confined to peninsular India, but there are other races with unspotted breasts in the north-east and Himalayas.

GREY-HEADED
FLYCATCHER
RED-BREASTED
FLYCATCHER
♀
♂
TICKELL'S
FLYCATCHER
♂
♀
HITE-BROWED
NTAIL
WHITE-SPOTTED
FANTAIL

SHAMA *Copsychus malabaricus.* 27cm. A shy inhabitant of ravines and forests in broken, hilly country; builds its nest in a clump of bushes or bamboo. Well-known as a cagebird it is popular for its fluty, mellow song. Resident in the Himalayas, N.E. India, Sri Lanka, and E. and W. Peninsular India.

MAGPIE-ROBIN *C. saularis.* 20cm. A common resident, widely distributed in hills and plains except in parts of Pakistan. Its favourite habitat of light woodland renders it a familiar garden bird, where it is the more welcome as it is a fine songster. The long tail is often held cocked up as it hops about on the ground, where it feeds on insects and beetles.

BLACKBIRD *Turdus merula.* 25cm. Resident in the Himalayas, and the hills of E. and W. Peninsular India and Sri Lanka. Although nesting up to high altitudes in the Himalayas and chiefly a forest bird, it is best known in the hill plantations or tea-gardens, where it hops about on the ground amonst the bushes. It has a fine, rich song, and a characteristic chuckling alarm call.

WHISTLING THRUSH *Myiophoneus caeruleus.* 33cm. A familiar bird along hill streams and ravines in the Himalayas, it bounds lightly over the boulders or stream bank on its long, strong legs. Like some other birds which live by rushing water, it has a shrill call-note, and a whistling song. The nest is placed under a bank, or by a waterfall.

BLUE ROCK THRUSH *Monticola solitarius.* 23cm. Confined as a breeding bird in our area to rocky slopes in Pakistan and the western and central Himalayas, it occurs very widely in winter as far south as Sri Lanka. Partial to open, boulder-strewn places, but also regularly around old forts, the neighbourhood of buildings, or even rocky roads in hill forest. Usually seen solitarily, it feeds on the ground, flicking down from the top of a large boulder as it spies a grasshopper below. It is often rather wary and difficult to approach.

STONECHAT *Saxicola torquata.* 14cm. A common winter visitor throughout the area except in the extreme south and Sri Lanka; it is also a breeding bird in the Himalayas. A lively, dumpy little bird, usually seen perched on the top of a bush, or on the stem of a maize or other plant, it frequents open or hilly country, fields or fallow land. Constantly flits down to the ground to pick up an insect, returning straight to its perch, where it sits upright, flicking its tail, and uttering the hard double call-note.

PIED BUSH-CHAT *S. caprata.* 13cm. More commonly distributed as a breeding bird throughout our area, including Sri Lanka, it frequents fields, and grassy or scrubby open country in the plains, and builds a cup-shaped nest of grass on the ground under shelter of a bank or tussock. Usually to be seen in pairs, it has a harsh, grating note.

INDIAN ROBIN *Saxicoloides fulicata.* 16cm. Common throughout the area, except in the higher Himalayas, it is a confiding and lively bird. It occurs in open country, cultivation, gardens or thin forest, and spends much time searching for insect life on the ground, holding the tail cocked up as it hops about.

INDIAN ROBIN

BLACK REDSTART *Phoenicurus ochruros.* 15cm. A breeding bird of stony upland slopes in the Himalayas, and found in winter around cliffs or buildings, in dry or open country, throughout the area except in Sri Lanka. The red tail is conspicuous as it is constantly quivered, and indeed the bird is always on the move, flitting down from a post to catch an insect, or hopping amongst the boulders.

BROWN ROCK-CHAT
Cercomela fusca. 15cm. Unlike most chats, both sexes are alike. Resident in the dry open country of north central India, it inhabits rocky ravines, dry earthy places and old ruins. It has a strong direct flight, and is constantly active.

PLUMBEOUS REDSTART *Rhyacornis fuliginosus.* 13cm. A characteristic and charming little bird of streams in the Himalayas, it is commonly seen perched on boulders, even in the roughest torrents. Ever on the move, flitting from rock to rock, or into the air to snap at a fly. When perched it is constantly wagging or fanning the tail.

△

BROWN HILL WARBLER *Prinia criniger.* 17cm. A neglected maize-field on a scrubby hill-side is a favourite haunt, and it likes to cling to the dead, swaying stem as it makes its wheezy and unimpressive attempt at singing. A hill resident from Baluchistan to Assam.

GREY-HEADED FLYCATCHER-WARBLER *Seicercus xanthoschistos.* 11cm. Common in woodland and gardens in the Himalayas. It hunts actively through the foliage, now and then fluttering out after an insect, or hovering to pick at a leaf. Often a member of mixed hunting parties.

BROWN CHIFFCHAFF *Phylloscopus collybita.* 12cm. Abundant in winter in northern India and Pakistan wherever there are bushes, tall rank vegetation or light woodland. It has a quiet, rather sad little note, and flicks its wings and tail as it searches the foliage.

TAILORBIRD *Orthotomus sutorius.* 13cm. A common bird of gardens or scrub-jungle throughout the area. Owes its name to its remarkable habit of stitching leaves together to form a support for the nest. Has a chipping note.

ASHY PRINIA *Prinia socialis.* 13cm. Frequents grassland, low herbage in scrubby jungle or field edges throughout the area. Often seen as it crosses from one patch of grass to another, with weak and uncertain flight. It has an incisive, buzzing note, and a rather jerky, fluttering song-flight.

INDIAN PRINIA *P. subflava.* 13cm. Found throughout the area in plains or foothills, in scrub, cultivation or dry grassland, even in arid areas. The long tail is frequently held up and flicked, and when in a small party the birds keep in touch with quiet clicking notes.

STREAKED FANTAIL WARBLER *Cisticola juncidis.* 10cm. Occurs in rich grassland, waterside herbage or crops throughout the area. Notable for its song-flight, when it circles overhead with undulating flight, making a sharp note.

CHIFFCHAFF
GREY-HEADED FLYCATCHER-WARBLER
TAILOR-BIRD
ASHY PRINIA
INDIAN PRINIA
STREAKED FANTAIL WARBLER

STREAKED LAUGHING-THRUSH *Garrulax lineatus*. 20cm. The laughing thrushes are hill forest birds, often shy and secretive, and keep to thick undergrowth and bushes. They are very gregarious, and the parties now and then break out into a medley of cackling laughter, drawing attention to their presence. The birds spend much time scratching about on the ground with their strong feet, searching for berries and insects, and are reluctant to fly when disturbed, but glide off downhill with bowed wings to dive into another patch of cover. The Streaked Laughing Thrush is a common Himalayan species, frequenting tangled ravines and thick scrub, and sometimes gardens at hill-stations.

WHITE-CRESTED LAUGHING-THRUSH *G. leucolophus*. 28cm. Common in forests and tangled undergrowth, and often difficult to see, although the flocks are much given to loud, explosive laughter. It occurs in the Himalayas from Himachal Pradesh eastwards.

WHITE-THROATED LAUGHING-THRUSH
G. alboqularis. 28cm. Very widely distributed from Afghanistan to Indo-China, and particularly common in the W. Himalayas. Tends to spend less time on the ground than some of its relatives.

JUNGLE BABBLER
T. striatus. 25cm. Very common, nicknamed "Satbhai" in Hindi, the flocks gather to drive away predators with much agitated flapping and noisy chattering. Found widely in the plains and foothills in light woodland or cultivation.

LARGE GREY BABBLER
T. malcolmi. 27cm. A common but rather local species, found in cultivated land or gardens in central and Peninsular India.

COMMON BABBLER *Turdoides caudatus.* 23cm. A plains bird, found throughout most of the area except Sri Lanka, the north-east and Bangladesh, in open, often dry country with scattered bushes and trees. Hops about under hedges in parties, and has a laboured flight.

YELLOW-EYED BABBLER
SCIMITAR BABBLER
YELLOW-BREASTED BABBLER
SPOTTED BABBLER
RUFOUS-BELLIED BABBLER

YELLOW-EYED BABBLER *Chrysomma sinense.* 18cm. Common in grassland, bushes, bamboo and scrub; it is found throughout the area, mostly in the plains, except in the dry areas of the north-west. Often in little parties, it hunts through the vegetation near the ground, the odd bird emerging now and again to cling briefly to a tall stem before disappearing again.

SLATY-HEADED SCIMITAR-BABBLER *Pomatorhinus schisticeps.* 20cm. A shy bird, inhabiting thick undergrowth, scrub and forest; it is common in the Himalayas, N.E. India, much of the E. and W. Peninsular, and Sri Lanka. Scimitar-Babblers are a distinctive group, having a long curved bill, a long tail and short rounded wings. They also have a characteristic hollow or fluty note with which they call to each other.

YELLOW-BREASTED BABBLER *Macronous gularis.* 13cm. A repeated, rather rich piping note in the undergrowth may draw attention to a party of these babblers, and like many other small birds they make a harsh churring noise when alarmed. They frequent bamboo brakes, scrub and undergrowth in forested areas in the plains and foothills of the N.E. Peninsular, and Central Himalayas to Bangladesh and Assam.

SPOTTED BABBLER *Pellorneum ruficeps.* 16cm. Rather shy and retiring, this babbler is sometimes glimpsed briefly as it hops over a bare patch by a path or under bushes, but often attracts attention by its repetitive whistling notes, or its rattling, churring alarm-note. It keeps close to the ground in bamboo jungle, scrub, forest or around tea-gardens, and is common in the hills of the W. and E. Peninsular and the north central parts of the Peninsular, the Himalayas and N.E. India.

RUFOUS-BELLIED BABBLER *Dumetia hyperythra.* 13cm. Common in Sri Lanka and throughout most of India except the north-west, it is a bird of thick vegetation or scrub. The members of a flock keep in touch with a quiet cheeping, but are often difficult to watch in the thick cover. The races in the western and southern Peninsular and Sri Lanka have the throat white.

BLACK-HEADED BABBLER *Rhopocichla atriceps.* 13cm. Very common in Sri Lanka and the lowland and hill forests of W. and S.W. India, it keeps to thick undergrowth in ravines and by streams in evergreen forest. In Kerala the local race has a sooty head while in Sri Lanka it has a black mask. Often in parties, it is constantly on the move, and the birds keep in touch with a continual low chittering or churring.

BLACK-HEADED BABBLER

QUAKER BABBLER
CHESTNUT-HEADED
TIT-BABBLER
YELLOW-NAP
YUHINA
PEKIN
ROBIN
NEPAL HOARY
BARWING
BAR-THROATED
SIVA

CHESTNUT-HEADED TIT-BABBLER *Alcippe castaneceps.* 10cm. Found from Nepal to Bhutan and Assam in undergrowth, bamboo and evergreen forest. Sociable and constantly active, it is very reminiscent of a tit in its actions as a party swings and searches through the twigs, clinging to the trunks or peering under leaves.

QUAKER BABBLER *A. poioicephala.* 14cm. Usually in small groups with mixed hunting parties, it gleans through the foliage, constantly uttering a low churring, and is not particularly shy. It is found in Peninsular India and Assam in forest and scrub.

YELLOW-NAPED YUHINA *Yuhina flavicollis.* 13cm. One of the commonest and most easily noticed of the small birds which flock through the wooded slopes of the Himalayas and the hills of Assam and Indo-China.

PEKIN ROBIN *Leiothrix lutea.* 14cm. More familiar as a cagebird, renowned for its rich warbling song, than as a wild bird, it is found in mountain forests from Nepal to Indo-China. It is inclined to keep to undergrowth in ravines, gulleys and steep slopes, and feeds mostly on or near the ground, so is difficult to watch.

NEPAL HOARY BARWING *Actinodura nipalensis.* 20cm. A fairly common and distinctive bird of Himalayan woodland, from Nepal eastwards. Often seen in company with laughing thrushes in one of the frequent hunting parties. Usually several birds keep close together as they move through the bushes, glades and clearings on a hillside.

BAR-THROATED SIVA *Minla strigula.* 14cm. Found commonly in the hill forests from the W. Himalayas eastwards, flitting through the foliage in small parties, which move across the hillside surprisingly fast.

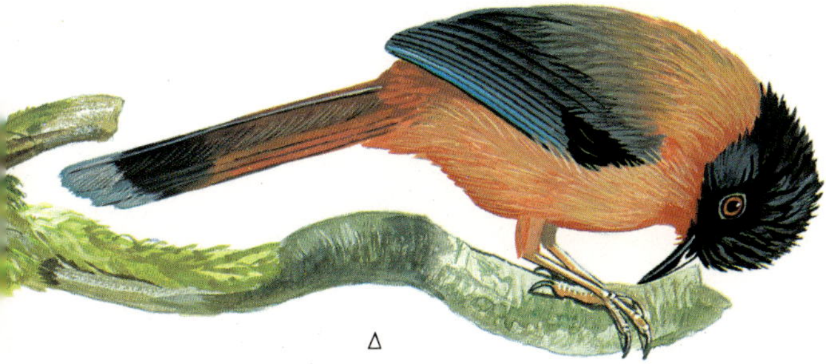

△

BLACK-HEADED SIBIA *Heterophasia capistrata.* 20cm. An attractive and lively inhabitant of the Himalayan forests, this is a familiar species round many of the hill stations, and is not particularly difficult to watch. A noisy bird with a loud, clear whistling note, and usually seen as it hunts actively through the branches of a tree, hopping lightly up the boughs, or clinging to the bark and twigs as it searches for insects.

YELLOW-CHEEKED TIT *Parus xanthogenys.* 13cm. A cheerful and lively member of the hunting parties so often seen in hill forests. It is found through most of the N. and N.E. and western parts of the Peninsular and in the Himalayas. It has the typically bright and ringing call-notes of the family, and is most active when searching through the foliage for insects, swinging upside down, and flitting lightly from one twig to the next.

GREY TIT *P. major.* 13cm. Widely distributed through the hills and plains, it shows much local variation in plumage. A bird of forest-edge, thickets, light woodland or gardens, often in company with other species. Nests in a hole in a tree, making a soft cup of moss, feathers and hair in which to lay the five or six eggs.

RED-HEADED TIT *Aegithalos concinnus.* 10cm. An enchanting little tit, often seen in active parties which follow each other through the bushes and trees, keeping in touch with a soft, buzzing call. Very alert and acrobatic, swinging about and creeping and fluttering through the twigs before flying off, one after the other, to the next bush. It has a dipping flight on rounded wings, and the long tail pumps up and down. A bird of open woodland and scrubby hillsides in the Himalayas.

HIMALAYAN TREE-CREEPER *Certhia himalayana.* 13cm. Tree-creepers spend much of their time scrabbling mouse-like up the bole of a tree, often going around it in spirals as they search for insects under the bark. On reaching the top, they fly down to the base of the next tree, to work their way upwards again. This species is found in the hills of Kashmir and western Nepal in coniferous forests, moving down to the adjacent area of plains in the winter. Two other species are quite common in the Himalayas.

CHESTNUT-BELLIED NUTHATCH *Sitta castanea.* 13cm. An even more adept climber than the creeper, it can move down a trunk headfirst, and has large, well-curved claws for grasping the bark. It taps the wood for grubs much like a woodpecker, and is often seen among the mixed hunting parties in woodland. It is found in either coniferous or deciduous forest in the Himalayas, much of northern and central India and Kerala.

VELVET-FRONTED NUTHATCH *S. frontalis.* 13cm. A bird of evergreen forests in the Himalayas, E. and W. Peninsular and Sri Lanka. Like other nuthatches, it nests in a hole, adjusting the size by plastering mud around the entrance. It is very active, and has a hard chipping note.

PURPLE SUNBIRD *Nectarinia asiatica.* 10cm. Found throughout the area, it is a familiar bird in gardens, although equally likely to be seen in semi-desert or thick forest, as long as there are trees and shrubs in flower. Feeds largely on nectar, but also takes small flies and other insects. Has a rapid, dashing flight, and constantly repeats a sharp call-note; also a good songster.

PURPLE-RUMPED SUNBIRD *N. zeylonica.* 10cm. Common in Peninsular India, Bangladesh and Sri Lanka. Always active, flitting from flower to flower, and making a quiet chirping note, it takes little notice of being watched. Builds a delicate, hanging nest.

▽

INDIAN WHITE-EYE *Zosterops palpebrosa.* 10cm. Found throughout the area in the hills or plains, wherever there are trees. It hunts actively through the foliage for insects much like a warbler, and has a thin, sibilant call-note. It is replaced in the hills of Sri Lanka by another species, *Z. ceylonensis*, similar but less yellow.

YELLOW-BACKED SUNBIRD
Aethopyga siparaja. 15cm. A forest bird, in the Himalayas, Bangladesh and Assam, and also in the north-east of the Peninsular and the Western Ghats. Although it visits gardens it is rather a shy bird, but like its relatives constantly active, flying rapidly amongst the blooms from which it takes the nectar. It has a clipped, sibilant call-note.

TICKELL'S FLOWERPECKER
Dicaeum erythrorhynchos. 9cm. Common in woodland throughout the area except in the arid parts of N.W. India and Pakistan. Feeds on the fruit of parasitic plants such as Lantana and Loranthus, thus spreading them wherever the seed is dropped. Has a sharp tinny note.

THICK-BILLED FLOWER-PECKER *D. agile.* 9cm. Often seen singly, flying high up between the tree-tops, uttering its metallic note. It occurs throughout the area except in Pakistan.

BLACK-HEADED BUNTING *Emberiza melanocephala.* 17cm. Breeding in western Asia and eastern Europe, it visits Pakistan and N.W. India in large numbers in winter. Flocks feed amongst the crops or on fallow ground, flying up into nearby trees or hedges when disturbed, the brightly coloured males being conspicuous. They do much damage in the grain-fields.

RED-HEADED BUNTING *E. bruniceps.* 17cm. Well known as a cagebird, it is a winter visitor to India, although not occurring as abundantly as the Black-headed Bunting. Frequents cultivation and fallow land in N.W., North and Peninsular India, keeping to the vicinity of scrub or bushes in which to roost or pass the heat of the day.

ROCK BUNTING *E. cia.* 15cm. Common in the W. Himalayas, it is a resident species, moving down to the valleys and foothills in winter. Found in clearings, or open grassy or rocky places and fields, it feeds on the ground on insects and seeds, flying up into nearby trees when disturbed. Makes a continual cheeping, and flicks the tail open, showing the white outer feathers.

COMMON ROSEFINCH *Carpodacus erythrinus.* 15cm. A migratory bird, it breeds in the Himalayas, and in winter ranges over the whole area to the south of the Peninsular. The flocks often consist mostly of females and young males, with only a sprinkling of rosy adult males. Frequents open countryside, fields and cultivation, feeding quietly on the ground on seeds.

RED-HEADED BULLFINCH *Pyrrhula erythrocephala.* 15cm. ▷ Resident in the Himalayas from Kashmir to Bhutan. A quiet bird, usually seen feeding in trees or bushes singly or in small parties. Moves about deliberately, and although not shy or difficult to watch, is not obtrusive. It has a low piping call, and breeds in the late summer.

HIMALAYAN GREENFINCH *Carduelis spinoides.* 14cm. Found in the mountains from Kashmir to Burma, it is familiar on the cultivated hillsides where it can find hemp or maize seeds in the terraced fields. Gregarious in winter, the flocks make a constant chirruping, and move about a good deal in their search for food. The cock has a pretty display flight, slowly flapping round with wings and tail spread.

RED AVADAVAT *Amandava amandava* 10cm. A popular and attractive cagebird. It frequents dense grass, sugarcane and reeds by swamps and jheels, and occurs throughout India and Bangladesh. The grass nest is domed, with a hole at the side, and is suspended in thick vegetation near the ground. This is the only species in its family in which the male has distinct breeding and non-breeding plumages.

GREEN AVADAVAT *A. formosa.* 10cm. Less well known, this munia has a more limited distribution, and only occurs locally in central India. It is found in flocks in grassland or in open forest country. Much remains to be learnt of its habits and behaviour in the wild; it is sociable when breeding, and constructs a nest resembling those of other munias.

SPOTTED MUNIA *Lonchura punctulata.* 10cm. Commonly found in flocks in areas of open scrub and cultivation, interspersed with grassland or gardens. It occurs throughout the plains and hills except in the drier parts of the north-west. It feeds in crops, and flies about in closely packed little groups, taking refuge in nearby bushes when disturbed. It breeds during the rains.

WHITE-BACKED MUNIA *L. striata.* 10cm. Found in the Himalayan foothills south to Bangladesh and N.E. India, and in Peninsular India and Sri Lanka. It is common in grassy areas in open forest. Usually seen in small flocks which feed on grass seeds on the ground, or perch amongst the flowering and fruiting panicles. They rise and fly off in typical straggling fashion when disturbed, to settle further away, each bird rising and falling in flight somewhat so that the flock seems to undulate.

WHITE-THROATED MUNIA *L. malabarica.* 10cm. A dull little bird, it has a wide distribution from the Himalayan foothills to Sri Lanka, Pakistan and Bangladesh. It makes a large oval nest in the grass, and this is also used for roosting purposes by several birds. It may sometimes be found nesting in a weaverbird colony. It occurs in rather dry scrub, and open or cultivated country.

BLACK-HEADED MUNIA *L. malacca.* 10cm. A familiar cagebird, known to aviculturalists as the Tri-coloured or Black-headed Nun. It is found in Bangladesh, Assam, S. Peninsular India and Sri Lanka. It haunts luxurious swampy grassland.

♀
♂
BAYA
♀
♂
STREAKED WEAVER
YELLOW-THROATED
SPARROW
♂
♀
BLACK-THROATED WEAVER

BAYA WEAVER *Ploceus philippinus.* 15cm. The bustling activity of a breeding colony draws attention to the marvellously woven grass nests hanging down from palm fronds or the branches of a tree. The long hanging entrance tunnels, up which the birds have to shoot in full flight, makes the nests virtually predator-proof. The males only acquire the yellow plumage and dark mask in the breeding season. Found throughout the area in plains, grasslands and cultivated areas.

STREAKED WEAVER *P. manyar.* 14cm. Widely distributed, but more a bird of reedbeds or tall, rank vegetation in swampy ground. The nest is differently constructed, as instead of being supported from one point on a bough, the top is attached to many plant stems which arch over, and give a more bunched and untidy appearance. Breeding takes place during the rains, as it does with all weavers.

BLACK-THROATED WEAVER *P. benghalensis.* 15cm. Colonies tend to be much smaller than those of the other two species – sometimes only five or six nests, and these are placed quite low down in vegetation and not suspended from trees. A common bird of damp grassland or cultivation, patchily distributed across N. India to Assam.

YELLOW-THROATED SPARROW *Petronia xanthocollis.* 14cm. A common, although not strikingly coloured resident species of open or cultivated country, light woodland or scrub, found throughout the area except in the higher Himalayas and Sri Lanka. It spends much time feeding on fields or tracks, often in flocks, flying up into the trees when disturbed. The nest is placed in a hole in a tree.

HOUSE SPARROW *Passer domesticus.* 15cm. This familiar and cheeky town dweller needs little introduction, being a common parasite on man throughout the area. It roosts communally in noisy chattering flocks in thick bushes or trees, and the untidy, shapeless nest is very often placed on a building. The large flocks which sometimes gather to raid crops or fruit can do considerable damage, and despite their familiarity with man, sparrows are always very wary and alert.

BRAHMINY MYNA *Sturnus pagodarum.* 22cm. A familiar bird around towns, it also frequents lightly wooded countryside far from habitation, and is found from the Himalayan foothills south across India to Sri Lanka. Although dependent on trees for nesting and roosting purposes and as songposts, it is, like most of its family, mainly a ground feeder, taking both animal and vegetable matter. It is also attracted to flowering or fruiting trees.

GREY-HEADED MYNA *S. malabaricus.* 20cm. Keeping more in the foliage of large trees, it is perhaps less easily noticed than some of its relatives. The flocks are, however, noisy and much in evidence at the blossoms of flowering trees, where they take the nectar, as well as searching for insects. Found in light forest or wooded countryside through Peninsular and N.E. India and the Himalayan foothills. The race in S.W. India, *S. m. blythii*, has the head and breast white.

PIED MYNA *S. contra.* 23cm. A conspicuous and common bird of the plains of N., N.E. and Central India, this myna is often to be seen in small parties feeding in fields or among cattle. Much addicted to the neighbourhood of villages and cultivation, it is less arboreal than the Greyheaded Myna, although placing its bulky nest in a tree.

ROSY STARLING *S. roseus.* 23cm. Highly sociable, and feeding in open country in large flocks, this very handsome starling is a winter visitor to N. and N.W. India and Pakistan. It migrates in large numbers through north-west Pakistan to and from its breeding grounds in western Asia, and takes a heavy toll of locusts on occasion.

COMMON STARLING *S. vulgaris.* 21cm. As a breeding bird, it is confined within our area to Kashmir and Sind, but its numbers are greatly augmented in winter by migrants, and the flocks then spread out over the plains of north and central India. The closely packed flight formation and restless, urgent manner of feeding are characteristic.

GREY-HEADED
MYNA
S. m. blythii
BRAHMINY
MYNA
S. m.
malabaricus
PIED
MYNA
imm
adult
ROSY STARLING

JUNGLE MYNA
BANK
MYNA
COMMON MYNA
HILL
MYNA

JUNGLE MYNA *Acridotheres fuscus.* 22cm. Found in well-wooded districts, often in hilly country, around villages and cultivation, although it is markedly less closely associated with man than the Common Myna. Frequently in family parties and small flocks, it feeds in the fields, and, like other mynas, can regularly be seen at the blossoms of flowering trees, from which it sips the nectar. Often in company with the Common Myna, it is probably sometimes overlooked as a distinct species. It nests in a hole in a tree or building. Found across northern India and the Himalayan foothills, and through western Peninsular India.

BANK MYNA *A. gingianus.* 21cm. Widely distributed across the dry plains of northern India from Pakistan to Calcutta, it is as dependent on man and his activities as is the Common Myna. A sociable, confiding bird, quite at home stealing scraps from a busy market, or running between the hooves of grazing cattle to snap up the flies. It nests in colonies or small groups in tunnels bored into earth cliffs.

COMMON MYNA *A. tristis.* 22cm. Perhaps the most widely known and abundant bird throughout the area, and especially familiar as it is so closely associated with man, whether in remote hill-villages, or in large towns. It has characteristics in common with the House Sparrow such as adaptability, opportunism and a lack of specialisation which enable it to be highly successful. Often seen hopping or running about on lawns or paths, the big white wing patches are suddenly prominent as it flies off. The untidy nest may be placed in any hole or ledge in masonry or trees, up to three broods being raised.

HILL MYNA *Gracula religiosa.* 28cm. Starlings and mynas are excellent mimics, and the expertise of this species at learning and repeating phrases of human speech has rendered it one of the most widely known and engaging cagebirds in the world. In the wild, it is a sociable bird of hill forests in S.W. India, Sri Lanka, the Himalayan foothills to Assam, and an area in the N.E. Peninsular. It is strictly arboreal, feeding on fruits and berries as well as nectar, and makes its nest in a tree-hole. Even in the wild state it is vocal, having a wide variety of whistles, and other mellow or harsh calls. A closely related species in Sri Lanka is described on page 158.

RED-BILLED
BLUE MAGPIE
TREE-PIE
BLACK-HEADED ORIOLE
♀
GOLDEN ORIOLE
♂

RED-BILLED BLUE MAGPIE *Urocissa erythrorhyncha.* 65cm with tail. This handsome magpie is fortunately not difficult to see around the hill resorts of the Himalayas, where it is common from Kashmir eastwards through Nepal. Often in small parties, the birds follow each other from one patch of woodland to another, flying over the valleys with the long tails arching conspicuously behind. They feed on a wide variety of animal or vegetable matter, even taking carrion. It is primarily a bird of moderate altitudes, where the woodland is interspersed with tea-gardens or terraced fields, and builds its small twig nest in bushes or trees. A similar, but yellow-billed species, *U. flavirostris*, lives at slightly higher elevations.

INDIAN TREE-PIE *Dendrocitta vagabunda.* 45cm. Found in wooded countryside, groves or gardens throughout the plains or foothills, except in Sri Lanka. Often in parties in the tree-tops, or with a hunting party or "bird-wave". It is noisy, with a range of loud, harsh calls, and also has a mellow and familiar whistle. Tree-pies feed on more or less anything from small birds and bats to figs or other fruit, and are inquisitive and bold, but always wary.

BLACK-HEADED ORIOLE *Oriolus xanthornus.* 25cm. Common throughout the area except in Pakistan, it keeps much to leafy trees and bushes in well-wooded country, gardens, parks and groves. Usually noticed as it flies from one tree to another, the gold plumage contrasting with the foliage, but also often detected by its fluty whistle. Orioles feed on fruit and insects, and suspend their hammock-like nest from twigs.

GOLDEN ORIOLE *O. oriolus.* 25cm. A common bird in Kashmir, it also breeds across northern India, wintering in the south and Sri Lanka. A somewhat active and restless bird, though when hunting through the foliage of large trees it is inconspicuous. However, it has a lovely fluty whistle which betrays its presence.

JUNGLE CROW *Corvus macrorhynchos.* 50cm. Very widely distributed from the treeless slopes of the high Himalayas throughout India and Sri Lanka. It is less of a town bird than the House Crow, and is most at home on the outskirts of villages and cultivation in wooded country. Often seen singly, although in the Himalayas flocks gather at high altitudes and perform aerial acrobatics over the lonely passes.

HOUSE CROW *C. splendens.* 45cm. Highly gregarious and abundant, it is, with the Common Myna, the most familiar bird in India. It ranges throughout the area, but is almost totally dependent on man's presence, and is to be found by the most remote village as regularly as it swarms around towns. It is, like the sparrow, bold and confiding, but also wary at the same time, ever ready to snatch a morsel of food, or flap quickly off at a hint of danger. The large stick nest is placed in a tree, and House Crows are frequently parasitised by Koels.

WHITE-BELLIED DRONGO *Dicrurus caerulescens.* 24cm. Found in light woodland or forest-edge in the plains and foothills throughout the area except in N.W. India and Pakistan. It has a variety of pleasant whistled notes, and is also a good mimic. Like other drongos, it behaves rather like a flycatcher, swooping out from its perch over a jungle path to capture a flying insect, or searching through the trees with a mixed hunting party. It is aggressive towards other birds which might constitute a threat to its nest or eggs, and the nest itself is a small cup made of fibres and lichens, and placed inconspicuously in a fork in a tree.

LARGE RACKET-TAILED DRONGO *D. paradiseus.* 35cm. A quick view of this drongo flying across a jungle clearing seems to reveal a medium-sized black bird being pursued by two tiny ones, as the "rackets" at the tail tip flap about with no visible connection. A noisy bird of mixed or evergreen forest throughout the area except in Pakistan and N.W. India.

BLACK DRONGO *D. adsimilis.* 30cm. A familiar, aggressive and active bird of open country or forest-edge. Often seen as it perches alertly on a post, ready to swoop out after an insect. It is a masterly flier when pursuing its prey or chasing off an intruder. Found throughout the area.

BLACK DRONGO

Synopsis of Families

With descriptions of 272 species not treated in main text

The illustrations in colour in this book show some 273 species of birds, which have been selected on the basis of relative abundance or familiarity. Most of them are widely distributed, although some are only locally common, in such areas as the Himalayas or in south-west India.

This summary lists all the families of birds occurring in the area, with the total number of species in each which have so far been recorded, together with brief descriptive details or an indication of status. The families are listed in the taxonomic sequence proposed by Dr K. H. Voous for Holarctic birds (Ibis 1973, 1977), which will be followed in the forthcoming Handbook of Birds of Europe, the Middle East and North Africa. It should be noted that this sequence has been modified in the main part of the text to allow for pictorial considerations.

Embodied in the synopsis are descriptions of 272 species for which there was no room in the main text, but which are either similar to species illustrated there, and mentioned here to avoid confusion, or are birds which are reasonably common or conspicuous where they occur. Where a family has representatives discussed in the main part of the text a page reference is given. As the plumage descriptions in this section are more detailed and use more technical terms, there is an explanatory diagram on page 161 which shows the topography of a bird and names the more prominent structural features and feather tracts.

Where more than one species in a genus is described, only the initial letter of the generic name is used after the first mention.

A somewhat rough and ready guide to distribution utilises the initial letters of the faunal regions as shown on page 10. Where the term P (Peninsular India) is used, it is not to be taken as excluding SW (Kerala and parts of adjoining states), unless the species concerned is not likely to find suitable habitat there – i.e. is perhaps a bird of dry plains. However, where SW is used it indicates that the bird concerned is more or less confined to the humid hills in that area. Note also that a number of species are restricted within N (Northern India) to the Himalayan foothills at up to around 1000m, although some may penetrate the Himalayas to some extent, eg to the Kathmandu valley. The distribution symbols must therefore be interpreted with discretion and due allowance for local anomalies.

How to use the Synopsis

If you are trying to identify a bird which does not seem to fit any of the coloured figures, the first thing to decide is to which family it is likely to belong. This should be possible by comparing the general look and structure of the bird with the colour plates where typical species from most families are shown. At least one species from all the more important families omitted from the main text is illustrated in this Synopsis, so if necessary a quick glance through the pictures from here on may be necessary. When you have narrowed down the possible families to one or two, read through the brief text in the main part of the book for clues as to habits and habitat; then search through the descriptions of other species in this section. The total number of species figure will give you an idea of how thoroughly the family is covered. The descriptions here are intended to point to diagnostic features and are not exhaustive accounts of all plumages. Remember that a bird may be moulting or be in a confusing immature dress. If in doubt take accurate notes – the more detailed the better. The ultimate reference work is the Handbook. It is quite often impossible to make a certain identification because of too brief a view, distance, bad light etc. DO NOT record a bird identified as to species in your notes unless it is possible to be quite certain.

DIVERS or **LOONS** Gaviidae. 2 species. Both extremely rare, only one winter record for each.

GREBES Podicipedidae. 4 species. P. 16
Great Crested Grebe *Podiceps cristatus.* 48cm. Dark brown above, white below. Long slender white neck; prominent chestnut and black 'ear-tufts' and ruff in summer, largely absent in winter. On inland or coastal waters in NW, N, and NE in winter.

Black-necked Grebe *P. nigricollis.* 33cm. Blackish-brown above in winter, top of head darker. White cheeks, throat and foreneck, breast and underparts. Slender tip-tilted bill. Jheels in winter in NW, N.

Great Crested Grebe **Black-necked Grebe**

Masked Booby

Redbilled Tropicbird

PETRELS and **SHEARWATERS** Procellariidae. 9 species. Oceanic birds, sometimes seen offshore. Rather few observations from Indian waters for most species, but probably under-recorded. **Wedge-tailed Shearwater** *Puffinus pacificus.* 48cm. Skims waves on stiff wings; flap and glide flight. Dark brown, tail wedge-shaped. Bill slender. Recorded so far off coasts of western seaboard.

Wedge-tailed Shearwater

STORM PETRELS Hydrobatidae. 3 species. **Wilson's Storm Petrel** *Oceanites oceanicus.* 18cm. Fluttering and gliding flight. Legs sometimes dangled, may show yellow webs of feet. All dark except white rump and dusky bar across upperwing. Tail square. Western and southern seaboards.

Wilson's Storm Petrel

TROPICBIRDS Phaethontidae. 3 species. Oceanic. Mostly white; central tail feathers elongated. Bills red or yellow. **Redbilled Tropicbird** *Phaethon aethereus.* 50cm plus 50cm tail streamers. Bill red, tail all white. Fine black barring on back; black wing tips and wing-bar. Strong flight on pointed wings, often screaming loudly, and chase each other like Swifts. Dive for fish or squids. So far recorded off western coasts, south of Sri Lanka.

BOOBIES Sulidae. 3 species. Large marine birds with long narrow wings and long tail, giving streamlined appearance. **Masked Booby** *Sula dactylatra.* 80cm. All-white except for black tail, and black tips and rear border to wing. Steady flap and glide flight; dive for fish. All-brown immature birds similar to those of the other species. Patchy intermediate plumages occur as white is gradually assumed.

CORMORANTS, SHAGS Phalacrocoracidae. 4 species. P. 16.

DARTERS Anhingidae. 1 species. P. 16.

PELICANS Pelecanidae. 3 species. Huge waterbirds with extensible skin pouch below long bill. Powerful fliers, often soaring. Sociable, often in large flocks where they occur. Fish from surface of water. **White Pelican** *Pelecanus onocrotalus.* 180cm. Rosy white plumage contrasts with black tips and rear border to wings, conspicuous in flight. Large bare facial patches and legs and feet pinkish. Breeds NW, on ground, wintering to P, N, and NE.

Dalmatian Pelican *P. crispus.* 180cm. Like White Pelican, but only wing-tips dusky-black, the wings lacking the broad black margin on underside. Secondaries dusky above. Legs and feet dark grey. Forehead feathers in this species and Spotbilled end in curved or concave line above base of bill, but in forward-pointing wedge in White Pelican. Winters on lakes or jheels in NW, N, and NE.

Spotbilled Pelican *P. philippensis.* 150cm. Plumage above and below markedly off-white or greyish; the lack of black in the wings and grey tail distinguish it from the other two species. Feet and legs dark grey. Row of small spots along upper mandible. Breeds colonially, but very locally, in trees, in southern P, NE and Sri Lanka, but more widespread in winter.

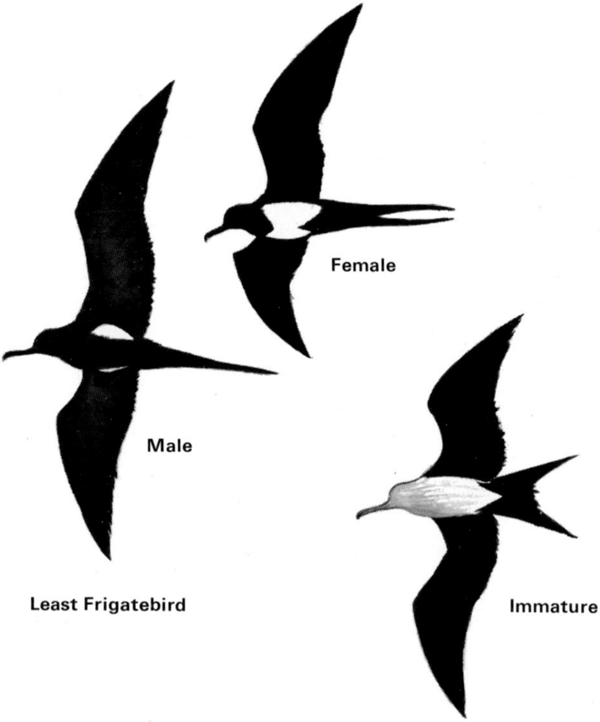

FRIGATEBIRDS Fregatidae. 2 species. Large blackish marine birds with angled, pointed wings and long forked tails. Piratical behaviour. Most records off western seaboard and Sri Lanka.
Least Frigatebird *Fregata ariel.* 80cm. Adult male all-black except white patch on each flank. In female white extends across lower breast. Immature browner above, head and underparts white lightly streaked brown, head sometimes brown. Nearest breeding station is Aldabra Island, off Madagascar. Recorded off Bombay.

HERONS, EGRETS and **BITTERNS** Ardeidae. 20 species. Pp. 18, 20. **White-bellied Heron** *Ardea insignis.* 125cm. A large grey heron, with crown, primaries and tail black. White throat and belly and underwing. Waterways and marshes in forested country in Himalayan foothills and NE. **Purple Heron** *A. purpurea.* 87cm. Darker, more slender and angular than Grey Heron. Sides of head and neck light chestnut, becoming richer and mixed with black on underparts. Purplish-blue above, blacker on wings and tail. Crown and striping on neck black. Throughout the area in reedbeds or jheels in the plains. **Large Egret** *Egretta alba.* 90cm. Resembles Little Egret but nearly twice the size – stately and angular. Feet black. Bill black when breeding, otherwise rich yellow. Plumes on back but not head or neck. Widespread. **Intermediate Egret** *E. intermedia.* 70cm. Feet black. Bill black when breeding, otherwise yellow, often dusky-tipped. Plumes on breast and back but no crest. Common and widespread. **Little Bittern** *Ixobrychus minutus.* 36cm. Male has blackish wings and back, contrasting in flight with large pale patch on wing coverts. Underparts buffy. Female browner, more streaked, less contrasty. Reedbeds, waterside vegetation in NW, N, and NE. **Chestnut Bittern** *I. cinnamomeus.* 38cm. Uniform chestnut, paler below. Female speckly on wing coverts and streaked below. Widespread, in waterside vegetation. **Black Bittern** *Dupetor flavicollis.* 58cm. Mostly slaty-black, buffy cheek patch. Female browner. Crepuscular. Widespread in swamps and reedbeds.

Egrets in winter plumage

STORKS Ciconiidae. 8 species. P. 22. **Black Stork** *Ciconia nigra.* 97cm. Glossy black head, neck, breast and all upperparts. White below from lower breast to under-tail coverts. Bill, legs and feet red. Immature browner where adult black. Winters in NW, N, and NE by marshes or rivers. **Black-necked Stork** *Xenorhynchus asiaticus.* 135cm. A huge white stork ▷ with bill, head and neck black, and black tail and broad bar across wing. Legs red. Widely distributed by marshes or jheels. **Lesser Adjutant** *Leptopilos javanicus.* 120cm. Like Adjutant, with heavy pale bill, but uniform blackish upperparts without grey wing-bar. Lacks neck pouch and white ruff. Mainly in NE, N, and Sri Lanka, by water or swamps.

IBISES and **SPOONBILLS** Threskiornithidae. 4 species. P. 24.

FLAMINGOS Phoenicopteridae. 2 species. P. 25. **Lesser Flamingo** *Phoenicopterus minor.* 100cm. Like Greater, but plumage deeper pink, and not only much smaller but less slender and sinuous. Bill black. Breeds by salt-pans in NW, wandering to N in winter.

SWANS, GEESE and **DUCKS** Anatidae. 42 species. Pp. 26, 28. All three species of swans very rare. **Greylag Goose** *Anser anser.* 80cm. Plain ashy head and pale forewing; remainder of plumage greyish except white uppertail coverts and dark tail bar. Bill, legs and feet pink. Wary wintering flocks on water in NW, N and NE. **Common Shelduck** *Tadorna tadorna.* 60cm. Red bill with large knob at base. Head, two bands on back and flight feathers black. Chestnut band round upper back and breast, remainder of plumage white. Wintering on water in NW, N and NE. **Fulrous Whistling Duck** *Dendrocygna bicolor.* 51cm. Similar to *javanica,* but patch above tail white, and wide yellowish-white collar around foreneck, Widespread but local. Most common on jheels in NE.

Mallard
♂
♀
Shelduck
Gadwall
♂
♀
Shoveler
♂
♀
Pochard
♂
♀
Wigeon
♂
♀
Tufted Duck
♂
♀
Garganey
♂
♀

Mallard *Anas platyrhynchos.* 60cm. Male has glossy green head, thin white collar and brown breast. Black upper and under tail-coverts. Female brown and speckled, with dark crown and eyestripe, and pale buff supercilium. Male has yellow bill, female's is brownish. Legs and feet orange. Winters on jheels in NW, N, and NE.

Gadwall *A. strepera.* 51cm. Sexes rather alike, similar to female Mallard but belly white, breast darker. Legs yellowish. Male has black patch above and below tail. Wing-patch white. Common in winter in NW, N, and NE; rarer in P. **Wigeon** *A. penelope.* 49cm. Male has reddish head with creamy crown, pink breast, grey back and flanks. White patch on forewing. Female like a darker female Teal. Common in winter in NW and N, less so in P and NE.

Garganey *A. querquedula.* 40cm. Male has broad white eyestripe across brown head. Breast brown; flanks and forewing pale. Female like female Teal. Very common and widespread in winter. **Shoveler** *A. clypeata.* 50cm. Large bill. Male has dark green head, white breast, chestnut belly and flanks. Female speckly brown. Quite common and widespread in winter.

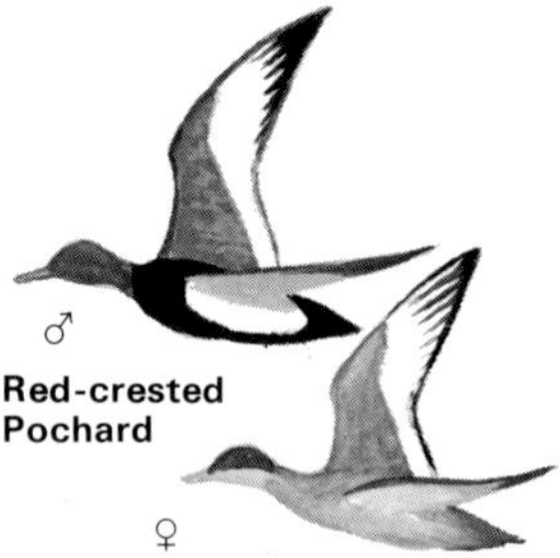

Red-crested Pochard

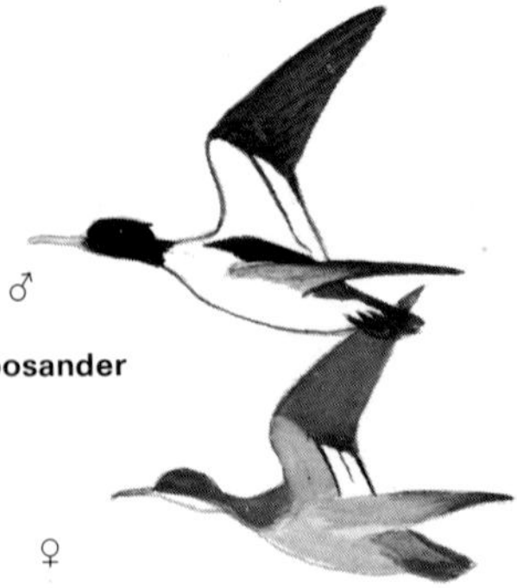

Goosander

Pochard *Aythya ferina.* 44cm. Chestnut head, black breast; light grey back and sides. Female duller. Dives frequently. Common in winter in NW and N, less so in NE and P. **Tufted Duck** *A. fuligula.* 44cm. Dumpy. Dives. Male all black except white wing-bar, belly and flanks. Female browner. Eye yellow. Winters in NW, N, NE, P; rarer in south. **Red-crested Pochard** *Netta rufina.* 54cm. Male has red bill, bright chestnut head, black breast. Back brown; flanks white contrasting with black breast, stern and belly stripe. Female has dark crown, whitish cheeks. Common on jheels in winter, except in southern P and Sri Lanka.

Goosander *Mergus merganser.* 62cm. Male has glossy black head and back. Primaries black. Pinkish flush on white underparts. Female has chestnut head and neck contrasting with white throat. Grey-brown above. Long, narrow red bill. Breeds H, to NE in winter. Rare in N, NW.

KITES, HAWKS, EAGLES, VULTURES and **HARRIERS** Accipitridae. 51 species. Pp. 30–36. **Brown Lizard Hawk** *Aviceda jerdoni.* 48cm. A crested, brownish hawk. Rufous breast, broad rufous barring on white underparts. Brown above with barred tail, and wings and tail barred below. Slow sailing flight on rounded wings above hill-forests in SW, Sri Lanka, and eastern H. **Crested Honey Buzzard** *Pernis ptilorhynchus.* 69cm. Common large hawk with long tail and wings, and small, slender head and neck. Very variable in plumage, but usually brown above with head grey. Underparts white to buff with, usually, heavy barring or blotching, or all brown. Underwing white with many dark, narrow bars, and well-barred underside of tail. Widespread in wooded country. **Crested Goshawk** *Accipiter trivirgatus.* 45cm. Round-winged woodland hawk with short crest. Brown above and white below. Adults have breast heavily streaked, rest of underparts and tail barred. Dark stripe down centre of throat. Immatures are streaked brown and white below. Soaring interspersed with stiff wing-flapping. SW and Sri Lanka, N, NE and H. **Besra Sparrowhawk** *A. virgatus.* 35cm. Very like Shikra, with heavier throat stripe, but its habitat is thick, often evergreen forest. SW and Sri Lanka, NE and H. **Long-legged Buzzard** *Buteo rufinus.* 60cm. Large, broad-winged hawk with ample, rounded, light rufous tail. Variable, but usually brown above; head and neck pale or white, and underparts whitish with belly brown. Birds which are all dark brown occur. Dark patch on bend of underwing contrasts with white patch on primaries, which are black-tipped. Soars over open country; looks lumpy when perched. Breeds H., winters to NW, N and NE.

Hodgson's Hawk-Eagle *Spizaetus nipalensis.* 72cm. Similar to Crested Hawk-Eagle, but larger, and a hill-forest species in H, NE, Sri Lanka and SW. **Black Eagle** *Ictinaetus malayensis.* 80cm. A large blackish eagle with long, faintly barred tail and long, rounded wings with secondaries bulging out so wing is narrower by body. Pale patch below primaries, cere and feet bright yellow against dark plumage. Soars above hill-forests; widespread. **White-bellied Sea-Eagle** *Haliaeetus leucogaster.* 70cm. White head, underparts and tail tip. Wings grey above and white below, with broad black border. Coastal waters from Bombay to Bangladesh and Sri Lanka. **Himalayan Griffon Vulture** *Gyps himalayensis.* 125cm. A huge, pale-sandy vulture of the high Himalayas, with blackish flight feathers and tail. **Pied Harrier** *Circus melanoleucos.* 47cm. Male has black head, back, breast, wing-tips and wing-bar. Rump white. Tail and wings silvery grey. Underparts white. Female closely resembles that of Pallid Harrier. Crops, marshes and fields in winter in NE and eastern and northern P to Sri Lanka. **Short-toed Eagle** *Circaetus gallicus.* 66cm. A large-headed eagle, white below with wings and tail barred. Wing-tips dark. Upperparts brown. Feeds largely on reptiles. Widespread in open country.

OSPREY Pandionidae. 1 species. **Osprey** *Pandion haliaetus.* 55cm. Dark brown above; face, neck and underparts white, with dark streak through eye and band of speckling across breast. Long, angled wings white below with usually prominent barring and a dark patch near the wing-bend. Catches fish by plunging into water. Widespread by lakes and rivers, or the coast.

FALCONS Falconidae. 12 species. P. 36. **Red-breasted Falconet** *Microhierax caerulescens.* 18cm. A tiny falcon. Face, collar and underparts white; throat and thighs rufous. Black eyestripe and upperparts. Forest edge in Himalayan foothills in N and NE. **Shahin Falcon** *Falco peregrinus.* 42cm. Like Laggar, but crown and a broad cheek-patch black. Dark browny-grey above, black-barred white underparts. Widespread on open hillsides.

MEGAPODE Megapodiidae. One species in the Nicobar Islands.

Blood Pheasant Snow Partridge

PARTRIDGES, QUAILS, PHEASANTS, TRAGOPANS, JUNGLEFOWL and **PEAFOWL** Phasianidae. 46 species. Pp. 38–45. **Snow Partridge** *Lerwa lerwa.* 38cm. Red bill and legs. Chestnut, streaked white, below. Barred black and white above. Alpine pastures in H. **Seesee Partridge** *Ammoperdix griseogularis.* 26cm. Pale pinky-grey above and below, darker streaking on flanks. Male has grey head with black and white eyestripe; female uniform pinky-brown. Arid foothills in NW. **Painted Bush Quail** *Perdicula erythrorhyncha.* 18cm. Red legs and bill. Chestnut below, flanks barred black and white. Throat white. Brown marked with black above. Grassy scrub in P. **Rufous-throated Hill Partridge** *Arborophila rufogularis.* 28cm. Throat and sides of neck rufous, sides of face white. Olive above with black spots and chestnut on wings. Breast grey. Scrub in H. **Painted Spurfowl** *Galloperdix lunulata.* 32cm. Blackish head and neck, chestnut back and flanks, all white-spotted. Female browner without white spotting. Skulks in thick scrub in P. **Ceylon Spurfowl** *G. bicalcarata.* 35cm. Throat white; head, neck, upper back and flanks blackish streaked white; lower back chestnut. Female browner with black barring. Forests in Sri Lanka. **Blood Pheasant** *Ithaginis cruentus.* 45cm. A short-tailed pheasant. Pale streaked plumage, grey above, light green below, with throat and streaks on breast red. Female rufous; both sexes have red legs. Forests and open scrub in H. **Western Tragopan** *Tragopan melanocephalus.* 70cm. Face, neck and breast red, rest of plumage blackish with paler markings and white spots. Female greyish-brown, spotted and streaked. Undergrowth in western H.

Ceylon Junglefowl *Gallus lafayetti.* 70cm. Like Red Junglefowl, which it replaces in Sri Lanka, but male has breast orange, not black. Widespread in jungle in Sri Lanka.

Koklas Pheasant *Pucrasia macrolopha.* 60cm. Streaky grey-brown above, chestnut below. Long, drooping crest; head metallic green with two pointed ear-tufts. Female mottled brown above, paler and streaky below. Forests in H. **Chir Pheasant** *Catreus wallichii.* 115cm (male). Long tail. Light browny-grey above, barred black. Long black crest. Paler below with dark flank markings. Female similar but smaller. Forests in H.

Chir Pheasant

Koklas Pheasant

BUSTARD-QUAILS Turnicidae. 3 species. P. 45. **Yellow-legged Bustard-Quail** *Turnix tanki.* 15cm. Light brown above with black speckling. Sandy-buff below, richer on breast, which is black-spotted at sides. Throughout area except Sri Lanka, in grassy places. **Indian Bustard-Quail** *T. suscitator.* 15cm. Upperparts brown, marked with buff, black and white. Buff underparts. Male has black barring on throat and breast. Female slightly larger and brighter; chin to centre of breast black, with black barring at sides. Grassland. Widespread.

CRANES Gruidae. 6 species. P. 46. **Siberian Crane** *Grus leucogeranus.* 150cm. A large, all-white crane, except for red face and black wing-tips. Pale browny bill and legs. Jheels in winter in NW and N.

RAILS, CRAKES, COOTS and **MOORHENS** Rallidae. 17 species. Pp. 50, 52. **Indian Banded Crake** *Rallina eurizonoides.* 25cm. Head, breast and upperparts rich uniform brown, flanks barred black and white. Bill and legs greenish. Waterside vegetation. Widespread.

Baillon's Crake *Porzana pusilla.* 19cm. Grey face, neck and breast. Brown above with small white flecks. Dark barring on flanks and vent. Waterside vegetation. Breeds Kashmir, widespread in winter.

FINFOOTS Heliornithidae. 1 species. A rare aquatic grebe-shaped bird with rather heavy yellow bill. Forest swamps, ponds or mangroves in NE.

BUSTARDS Otididae. 6 species. P. 48.

JACANAS Jacanidae. 2 species. P. 52.

PAINTED SNIPE Rostratulidae. 1 species. P. 53.

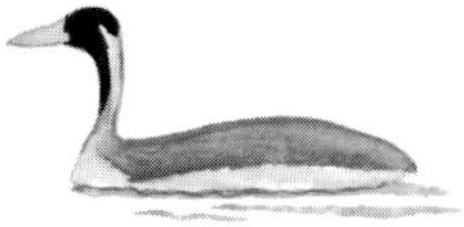

Finfoot

OYSTERCATCHERS Haematopodidae. 1 species. **Oystercatcher** *Haematopus ostralegus.* 42cm. Large, rather chunky shorebird with stout rather long, straight red bill. Black head, breast and upperparts. White below, on base of tail, and broad white wing-bar. Legs pink. Sociable and noisy. Winters on western coasts south to Sri Lanka.

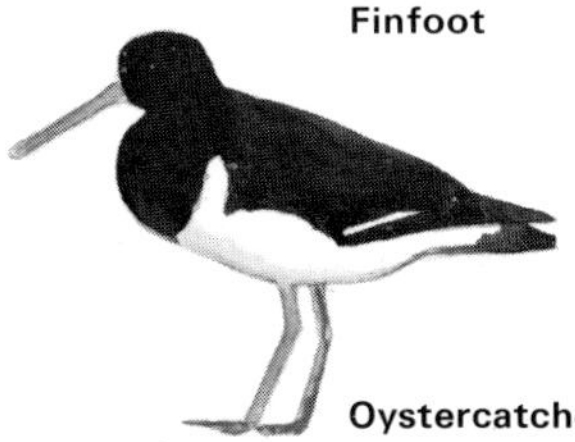

Oystercatcher

IBISBILL Ibidorhynchidae. 1 species. **Ibisbill** *Ibidorhyncha struthersii.* 40cm. A grey shorebird. Crown, face and a prominent breast – band black. White wing-bar and underparts. Long red down-curved bill. Breeds by stony streams in H, wintering to foothills in NE.

Ibisbill

STILTS, AVOCET Recurvirostridae. 2 species. P. 58.

CRAB PLOVER Dromadidae. 1 species. **Crab Plover** *Dromas ardeola.* 40cm. Large white shorebird with black back and flight feathers. Rather short heavy black bill. Long bluish-green legs. Winters on western seaboard south to Sri Lanka (where resident?).

STONE-CURLEWS Burhinidae. 2 species. P. 58. **Great Stone Curlew** *Esacus recurvirostris.* 50cm. Like a larger Stone Curlew, with heavier bill. Black face patches, unstreaked breast. Dry riverbeds; widespread.

COURSERS and **PRATINCOLES** Glareolidae. 5 species. P. 58. **Large Indian Pratincole** *Glareola pratincola.* 24cm. Brown above. Forked black tail with white base, black flight feathers. Buffy throat with narrow black border. Wing-lining chestnut (often hard to see). Dry open ground; widespread.

PLOVERS Charadriidae. 18 species. P. 54. **Spur-winged Lapwing** *Vanellus spinosus.* 30cm. Black crown and crest. Throat, primaries and tail-tip black. Pale grey-brown above and on breast. Underparts, patch above tail and wing-bar white. Black belly patch. River banks in N, NE and northern P. **Grey Plover** *P. squatarola.* 30cm. Speckled greyish above in winter, white below with black 'armpits' obvious in flight. Chin to belly and flanks black in summer. Common wintering bird on coasts. **Lesser Sand Plover** *Charadrius mongolus.* 19cm. Like Great, but bill slighter. In summer shows more extensive rufous breast-band and black forehead. Both species associate. Common on coasts in winter.

SANDPIPERS, SNIPES, CURLEWS ETC. Scolopacidae. 39 species. P. 56. **Whimbrel** *Numenius phaeopus.* 43cm. Like a smaller Curlew, but bill shorter and straighter. Dark stripes on crown. Coasts in winter. **Black-tailed Godwit** *Limosa limosa.* 45cm. Large shorebird with long, straight bill. Grey-brown above in winter, white below and base to black tail. Conspicuous white wing-bar. Long greyish legs. Marshes and coastal mud-flats, most common in NW and N. **Bar-tailed Godwit** *L. lapponica.* 38cm. Similar to Black-tailed but lacks wing-bar. Bill slightly tip-tilted, legs a bit shorter. Tail barred. Western coasts to Sri Lanka, rarer in the south. **Redshank** *Tringa totanus.* 28cm. Brown back and breast. White rear edge to wing obvious in flight. Legs red. Breeds Kashmir. Common at coasts and waterside in winter. **Greenshank** *T. nebularia.* 36cm. Larger and paler than Redshank. Wings all dark, long white rump patch; legs green. Triple call. Marshes and coasts in winter. **Turnstone** *Arenaria interpres.* 22cm. Stocky, with short orange legs. Dark brown above with white wing-bars, rump and underparts. Looks very pied in flight. Coasts in winter. **Pintail Snipe** *Gallinago stenura.* 27cm. Very like Common Snipe, but lacks white trailing edge to wing. In hand, shows eight outer tail feathers very thin and pointed. Widespread in marshy places in winter. **Sanderling** *Calidris alba.* 19cm. Pale grey above and white below in winter, with blackish shoulder patch and white wing-bar. Dark, straight bill. Runs actively. Common on coasts in winter. **Dunlin** *C. alpina.* 19cm. Like dark winter Little Stint, but larger; breast more streaked. Longer bill curves down slightly at tip. Pale wing-bar. Black belly patch in summer. Common on coasts throughout in winter, except Sri Lanka. **Curlew-Sandpiper** *C. ferruginea.* 20cm. Very like Dunlin in winter, but rump white. Legs and bill slightly finer and longer. Underparts all chestnut in summer. Coasts in winter. **Ruff** *Philomachus pugnax.* 29cm. Shortish, straight bill. Rather thin neck and small head. Neatly patterned upperparts; rump and centre of tail dark; narrow, pale wing-bar. Legs orange. Marshes and coasts in winter.

Grey Plover
Winter
Whimbrel
Crab
Plover
Dunlin
Winter
Redshank
Sanderling
Winter
Turnstone
Winter
Ruff
Winter
Black-tailed Godwit
Winter

Little Tern

Arctic Skua

SKUAS Stercorariidae. 3 species. Piratical gull-like birds. **Arctic Skua** *Stercorarius parasiticus*. 48cm. Adults have pointed elongated central tail-feathers. White flash on wing. Immatures and dark-phase adults all dark brown. Light phase brown above with dark cap. Yellowish-buff below with dusky breast-band. Chase other seabirds and retrieve dropped food. Offshore along NW coasts.

GULLS Laridae. 8 species. P. 60. **Great Black-headed Gull** *Larus ichthyaetus*. 70cm. A huge gull; pale grey above, white below. Head and neck black in summer, white with black streaks in winter. Heavy yellow bill with black patch. Widespread but not numerous by coasts or rivers, in winter. **Slender-billed Gull** *L. genei*. 42cm. Rather long red bill, yellow in winter. Pale grey wings and back; white head and underparts. Wing pattern resembles that of Black-headed. Breeds coastal NW, wintering along coast to Bombay. **Herring Gull** *L. argentatus*. 60cm. White head and body; mantle and wings grey, the latter with black tips. Bill yellow with red patch on lower mandible. Legs yellow or pink. Immature birds brown or brownish-grey, paler and streaked below, more heavily marked above. Bill black, or browny with black tip. Adults may show much variation in shade of mantle; may approach the slaty-black of Lesser Black-backed Gull which is otherwise similar. Both species winter along western seaboard south to Sri Lanka and irregularly but widely inland in NW, N, NE and H.

TERNS Sternidae. 21 species. P. 60. **Gull-billed Tern** *Gelochelidon nilotica*. 38cm. Like River Tern, but bill short, stout and black. Tail rather short and not deeply forked. Grey above, the tail and rump pale grey. Head very white in winter with black streaks on nape and patch behind eye; black cap in summer. Legs black. Breeds NW, common by coastal or inland waters in winter.

Caspian Tern *Sterna caspia.* 50cm. A huge tern with very large, heavy red bill. Legs and feet black. Pale grey above, but primaries dark underneath, noticeable in flight. Black head heavily streaked with white in winter. Breeds NW and Sri Lanka; widespread in winter. **Swift Tern** *S. bergii.* 50cm. White forehead, black crown and crest. Dark silvery-grey back and wings. Heavy greeny-yellow bill. Breeds on coastal islands off NW and NE, also off western P. and Sri Lanka; more widely around coasts in winter. **Lesser Crested Tern** *S. bengalensis.* 40cm. Resembles Swift Tern, but mantle paler and bill bright orange. Lacks the large white forehead patch. Quite common in coastal waters, especially in winter. May breed NW. **Little Tern** *S. albifrons.* 24cm. Very small; rapid flight, on narrow wings. Noisy. Forehead white; bill yellow with black tip. Legs yellow. Breeds NW and Sri Lanka; non-breeding or wintering birds widespread by coastal or inland waters.

SKIMMERS Rynchopidae. 1 species. **Indian Skimmer** *Rynchops albicollis.* 40cm. Tern-like, with very long narrow wings but short tail. Black cap separated from black upperparts by white collar. Prominent orange bill with lower mandible longer than upper. 'Ploughs' water with bill in flight. Widespread but local by rivers; not in southern P. or Sri Lanka.

Indian Skimmer

SANDGROUSE Pteroclididae. 8 species. P. 58. **Painted Sandgrouse** *Pterocles indicus.* 28cm. Sandy-yellow, closely barred black on tail, belly, wings and back. Brown and white band below breast. White forehead with broad black border. Female duller and more uniform, with barred breast. Widespread in open, stony scrub.

PIGEONS and **DOVES** Columbidae. 30 species. P. 62 **Grey-fronted Green Pigeon** *Treron pompadora.* 28cm. Male has large chestnut patch on back. Light green below, breast pinker. Forehead and crown grey. Female lacks chestnut, but both sexes have slaty-grey tail with green central feathers. Forests, widespread. **Orange-breasted Green Pigeon** *T. bicincta.* 29cm. Male has green head and back; mauve and orange patch on breast. Female is mostly yellow-green, but both sexes have the tail all slaty-grey. Forests, widespread. **Green Imperial Pigeon** *Ducula aenea.* 43cm. Large and heavy. Dark green above, light browny-grey below. Chestnut under-tail coverts. Forests, widespread. **Maroon-backed Imperial Pigeon** *D. badia.* 47cm. Head and underparts greyish, pale buff under tail. Upperparts deep coppery-brown. Forests in NE and SW and eastern H.

Snow Pigeon *Columba leuconota.* 34cm. White neck, breast and underparts, rump and base of tail. Head black, upper back brownish; wings grey with 3 dark bars. Rocky places in H. **Speckled Wood Pigeon** *C. hodgsonii.* 38cm. Head, neck and breast ashy, maroon-tinged, belly dark grey. Upperparts rich purply-brown, white-speckled on shoulder. Forests in H and NE. **Nilgiri Wood Pigeon** *C. elphinstonii.* 42cm. Grey head and underparts. Black and white chequered neck patch. Upperparts rich purply-brown. Forests in SW. **Ceylon Wood Pigeon** *C. torringtoni.* 36cm. Like Nilgiri Pigeon, but dark grey above, except deep pinkish-grey upper back, head and underparts lilac. Hill forests in Sri Lanka. **Rufous Turtle Dove** *Streptopelia orientalis.* 33cm. Bright reddish-brown above with dark chequering. Black and white neck patch; grey or white border to tail. Breeds H and eastern P, widespread in winter except Sri Lanka. **Emerald Dove** *Chalcophaps indica.* 27cm. Small, fast-flying dove, often seen on forest roads or clearings. Dark green above with whitish bands across lower back. Pinkish underparts and chestnut underwing. Red bill. Widespread except NW.

PARAKEETS and **LORIKEETS** Psittacidae. 15 species. P. 64. **Red-breasted Parakeet** *Psittacula alexandri.* 38cm. Bright green; grey head with black throat stripe, breast pink. Long tail. No red on shoulder. Male has red bill, female black. Light jungle in N and NE.
Slaty-headed Parakeet *P. himalayana.* 40cm. Dark grey head. Bright green above and below, with red shoulder patch, which female lacks. Long yellow-tipped tail. Forests or cultivation in H and NE.
Blue-winged Parakeet *P. columboides.* 38cm. Wings and yellow-tipped tail blue. Head, back and breast dove-grey, with black and blue collar. Bill red. Female duller with blackish bill. Western and southern P.
Layard's Parakeet *P. calthorpae.* 32cm. Similar to Blue-winged, but wings and breast green. Confined to Sri Lanka, mostly in hill woods.
Ceylon Lorikeet *Loriculus beryllinus.* 14cm. Like Indian, but crown and rump red, orange patch on upper back. Common in woodland; confined to Sri Lanka.

CUCKOOS, MALKOHAS, COUCALS Cuculidae. 22 species. P. 66.
Large Hawk Cuckoo *Cuculus sparverioides.* 38cm. Like a large Brainfever Bird but rich brown above. Breeds in woods in H and NE at higher altitudes, wintering widely as far as southern P.
Indian Cuckoo *C. micropterus.* 33cm. Dark brownish-grey upperparts, head and breast. White below with widely spaced broad black

bars. Black subterminal band on upperside of tail. The four-note call is familiar and unmistakable, 'ko-ko-ta-ko'. Common and widespread in woodland. **Cuckoo** *C. canorus.* 33cm. Similar to Indian Cuckoo, but underparts more closely and narrowly barred. Familiar two-note call. Breeds H, in winter throughout area except Sri Lanka. **Bay-banded Cuckoo** *Cacomantis sonneratii.* 24cm. Bright reddish-brown above, whitish below, all with wavy dark barring. 4-note call. Widespread in woodland, to Sri Lanka. **Indian Drongo-Cuckoo** *Surniculus lugubris.* 25cm. All black, except white barring on under tail-coverts. Tail forked. Resembles Drongo but less active; cuckoo-type flight. Widespread in woodland except NW. **Small Green-billed Malkoha** *Rhopodytes viridirostris.* 40cm. Long tail with white tips. Plumage oily greeny-grey, browner below. Light green hooked bill. Skulks in thickets. P and Sri Lanka. A similar but larger species, R. tristis, occurs in H and NE. **Sirkeer Cuckoo** *Taccocua leschenaultii.* 42cm. Large dark tail with white tips. Brown above with dark streaks, paler and streaked below. Bill red, yellow-tipped. Widespread in scrub. **Red-faced Malkoha** *Phaenicophaeus pyrrhocephalus.* 45cm. Glossy blackish plumage, white belly and flanks. Light green bill, bare red face. Forest in Sri Lanka; very rare in SW India. **Ceylon Coucal** *Centropus chlororhynchus.* 43cm. Like small Common Coucal but bill green. Scrub and woods in Sri Lanka. **Lesser Coucal** *C. toulou.* 34cm. Like a much smaller Common Coucal. Keeps to tall grass near jungle or wet areas in lowlands. Widespread except in Pakistan and Sri Lanka.

BARN and **GRASS OWLS** Tytonidae. 3 species. **Barn Owl** *Tyto alba.* 35cm. Pale buff above with fine grey stippling and delicate black and white spotting. White facial disk. White below, finely dark-spotted. Roosts by day in ruins, wells or buildings. Widespread, but rare in Sri ▷ Lanka.

OWLS Strigidae. 26 species. P. 68. **Forest Eagle Owl** *Bubo nipalensis.* 63cm. Like Eagle-Owl, but eyes brown, and underparts spotted rather than streaked. Forests in N, H, NE, south and west P and Sri Lanka. **Dusky Horned Owl** *B. coromandus.* 58cm. Rather uniform sooty plumage, lightly marked. Yellow eyes. Widespread in woodland; not in Sri Lanka. **Barred Owlet** *Glaucidium cuculoides.* 23cm. Like a larger Jungle Owlet, but closely barred whitish and dark brown. Woodland in NW, N, NE and H. **Brown Wood Owl** *Strix leptogrammica.* 50cm. Large, with no ear tufts. Prominent white eyebrows and whitish facial disk. Dark patches around eyes. Mottled brown above, paler and barred below. Widespread in woodland. **Mottled Wood Owl** *S. ocellata.* 48cm. Like Brown, but more rufous and heavily mottled and barred. Closely barred facial disk. Light woodland in NW, N, NE and P.

FROGMOUTHS Podargidae. 2 species. Resemble heavy-billed Nightjars. Nocturnal. Thick forests, one species in SW and Sri Lanka, the other in eastern H and NE, illustrated here.

Hodgson's Frogmouth

NIGHTJARS Caprimulgidae. 8 species. P. 70. Only four species are really widespread, but all are nocturnal and best told by their calls. There is a key to these in the Handbook, Vol. 4, page 8.

SWIFTS and **SWIFTLETS** Apodidae. 15 species. P. 70. **Himalayan Swiftlet** *Collocalia* ▷ *brevirostris.* 14cm. Slender, with shallow tail fork. Fluttery flight. Brown above with paler rump; light brown below. H and NE. **Edible-nest Swiftlet** *C. unicolor.* 12cm. Very similar to Himalayan but rump not paler than back. Gregarious and common by caves or cliffs in western P. and Sri Lanka. **White-rumped Swift** *Apus pacificus.* ▷ 18cm. Like a larger House Swift, but tail forked. Breeds H and NE, wanders widely in P.

TREE-SWIFTS Hemiprocnidae. 1 species. P. 70.

TROGONS Trogonidae. 3 species. **Indian Trogon** *Harpactes fasciatus.* 30cm. Short, broad bill; long, square-ended tail. Sits upright in forest trees and flycatches; rather a quiet and inactive bird. Head and breast black. White line on breast divides black from bright red underparts. Back yellowish-brown. Wings black with fine wavy white barring. Long black tail has white edges. Female has dark brown head and cinnamon underparts, and brown barring on wings. Forests in P and Sri Lanka.

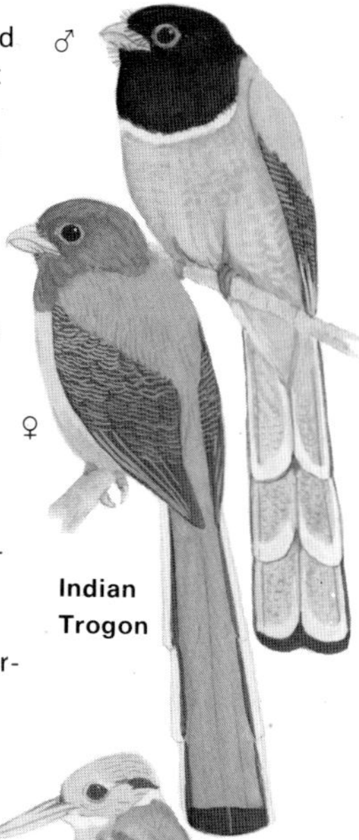

Indian Trogon

KINGFISHERS Alcedinidae. 12 species. P. 72. **Three-toed Kingfisher** *Ceyx erithacus.* 13cm. Tiny. Dark wings, shining amethyst back. Head and underparts orange-buff. Bill red. Widespread by jungle streams. **Brown-headed Storkbilled Kingfisher** *Pelargopsis capensis.* 38cm. Huge, with heavy red bill. Head and underparts brown or buffy. Back, wings, rump and tail bright blue. Widespread by water. Another species, *P. amauroptera*, very similar but with wings and tail brown, and only back and rump bright blue, occurs in coastal NE. **Black-capped Kingfisher** *Halcyon pileata.* 30cm. Red bill and white wing-patch. Black head, orange-buff underparts. Back and tail dark, brilliant blue. Throat, breast and collar white with rusty tinge. Coastal areas and swamps; widespread. **White-collared Kingfisher** *H. chloris.* 25cm. Head and back turquoise; white collar and underparts. Bill black. Coastal areas in NE; rare in western P.

Three-toed Kingfisher

Black-capped Kingfisher

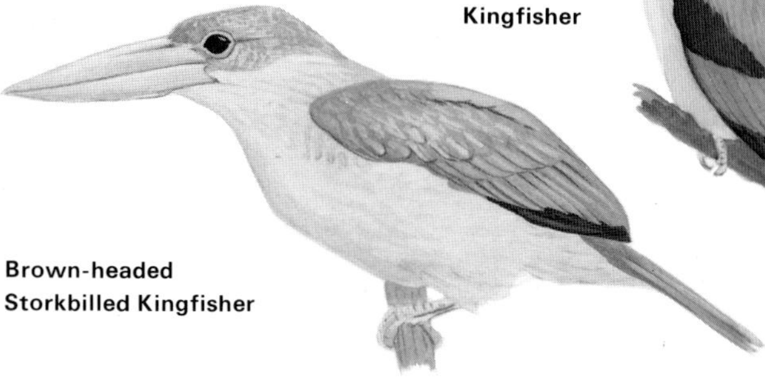
Brown-headed Storkbilled Kingfisher

BEE-EATERS *Meropidae.* 6 species. P. 72. **European Bee-Eater** *Merops apiaster.* 27cm. Underparts blue-green. Back chestnut with yellowish shoulder patches. Primaries blue, tail blue-green. Black eye-stripe and thin black necklace round yellow throat. Common breeder in Kashmir; occurs sporadically through NW. **Blue-cheeked Bee-Eater** *M. superciliosus.* 30cm. Green rump and tail distinguish it from Blue-tailed. Resident in dry, open areas in NW. **Blue-bearded Bee-Eater** *Nyctiornis athertoni.* 35cm. Bright green head and upperparts. Shaggy bright blue centre of throat and breast. Belly buffy and streaky; underside of tail yellow, dusky-tipped. Tail square-ended. Forests in H, N, NE and western P.

ROLLERS Coraciidae. 3 species. P. 74. **Kashmir Roller** *Coracias garrulus.* 30cm. Bright rufous-chestnut back and uniform turquoise head and underparts distinguish from Indian Roller. Breeds Kashmir; winters further west. **Broad-billed Roller** *Eurystomus orientalis.* 30cm. Dark oily blue-green plumage, but looks mostly blackish in flight, with an obvious round, pale patch on the primaries. Bill short, broad and red. Often sits exposed on tall dead forest trees. Forests in H, N, NE and SW. Probably extinct in Sri Lanka.

HOOPOE Upupidae. 1 species. P. 74.

HORNBILLS Bucerotidae. 8 species. P. 74. **Indian Pied Hornbill** *Anthracoceros malabaricus.* 85cm. Yellow and black bill with high casque. Black plumage with white wing-tips and corners of tail; underparts white. Woodland in N and NE. **Malabar Pied Hornbill** *A. coronatus.* 90cm. Like Indian but edges to tail all white. Woodland in P and Sri Lanka. **Malabar Grey Hornbill** *Tockus griseus.* 60cm. Like Grey, but lacks a casque on the bill. Tail all black with white corners. Woodland in western P and Sri Lanka.

HONEYGUIDES Indicatoridae. 1 species. Rare in H.

BARBETS Capitonidae. 10 species. P. 76. **Great Barbet** *Megalaima virens.* 33cm. Large pale yellow bill. Blackish head and throat. Breast and mantle dark brownish, underparts pale yellowish with dark streaking. Red under-tail coverts. Wings, back and tail green. Call is a loud plaintive double whistle 'Pee-yiaow', endlessly repeated. Forests in H and NE. **Lineated Barbet** *M. lineata.* 28cm. Like Green Barbet, but with broad pale streaking and much smaller eye-ring. Call much as in Green. Woodland in N and NE. **Small Green Barbet** *M. viridis.* 23cm. Bright green above, paler below. Head brown, throat and a broad line across ear-coverts white. Double note call. Western and southern P. **Yellow-fronted Barbet** *M. flavifrons.* 22cm. Dark green above, paler below. Yellow forehead; face and throat light blue. Sri Lanka, especially common in hill forests. **Crimson-throated Barbet** *M. rubricapilla.* 17cm. Resembles Coppersmith, but chin to breast crimson. Race in Sri Lanka has throat, eye-patch and supercilium golden. Forests in SW and Sri Lanka.

WOODPECKERS Picidae. 32 species. P. 76. **Wryneck** *Jynx torquilla.* 18cm. Superficially grey-brown, but plumage finely mottled and vermiculated above with irregular dark band up centre of back, bordered paler. Paler below, barred on throat. Rather long rounded tail with speckly cross-bars. Breeds H. Winters in light woodland in NW, N, NE and western P. **Speckled Piculet** *Picumnus innominatus.* 10cm. Tiny, woodpecker-like. Tail short and rounded. Olive above; whitish below with black spotting and barring. White face crossed with two dark bands. Often in hunting parties in low bushes. H, N, NE, P.
The typical woodpeckers are divided here for simplicity into 4 groups. (A) Those with plumage either rufous, buff black or grey – 5 species. **Rufous Woodpecker** *Micropternus brachyurus.* 25cm. Uniform chestnut, with dark barring on upperparts. Male has red patch below eye. Widespread except NW. (B) Those with green backs, often scarlet crown, and two with large yellow crests – 5 species. **Little Scaly-bellied Green Woodpecker** *Picus myrmecophoneus.* 29cm. Red crown in male. Green above, yellower on rump. Pale greenish-white below with dark scaly markings. Widespread except in NW. **Black-naped Green Woodpecker** *P. canus.* 32cm. Red crown in male. Black nape, face grey with black stripe from bill. Green above, dull pale greenish below. H, NE. **Small Yellow-naped Woodpecker** *P. chlorolophus.* 28cm. Golden crest and nape. Forehead red in male. Bright green above, barred pale brown and white below. Widespread except in NW. (C) Those with golden or red backs, mostly similar to the Golden-backed Woodpecker – 6 species.

Black-backed Woodpecker *Chrysocolaptes festivus*. 29cm. Shoulder patches golden. Black stripe running from eye encircles white upper back. Crest red in male, yellow in female. White below with black streaks on throat and breast. N, P and Sri Lanka. **Large Golden-backed Woodpecker** *C. lucidus*. 33cm. Scarlet crown in male, nape white. Golden back, rump red. Face white with black stripes; underparts white with dark scaly pattern. H, NE, N, western P and Sri Lanka. (D) Those with black and white barring or spotting on back, mostly similar to the Mahratta Woodpecker – 13 species. **Kashmir Pied Woodpecker** *Dendrocopos himalayensis*. 25cm. Black back with white shoulder patches and barring on wings. Face white with black stripes, and stripe over eye. Crown red in male. Buffy white below, red under tail. Western H. **Brown-fronted Pied Woodpecker** *D. auriceps*. 20cm. Forehead brown, crown streak yellow with red tip. White barring on blackish upperparts. White below, streaked with black. Pink under tail. Female lacks crown streak. H. **Brown-crowned Pygmy Woodpecker** *D. nanus*. 13cm. Small, barred brown and white above, with white stripe over eye. Dirty white, streaked darker, below. Male has red on hind crown. Widespread to Sri Lanka.

BROADBILLS Eurylaimidae. 2 species. **Long-tailed Broadbill** *Psarisomus dalhousiae*. 27cm. A rather sluggish but sociable arboreal bird. Large head and long tail. Bill light green. Face and throat deep yellow. Head black with two yellow patches and blue crown stripe. Mantle, back and underparts bright green. Tail blue. Wings blue and black showing white patch below. H (and foothills in N) and NE in evergreen forest. **Collared Broadbill** *Serilophus lunatus*. 18cm. Short drooping crest; tail short and graduated. Grey-brown above, chestnut on lower back. Tail black, white tipped. Wings black, blue and chestnut. Female has silvery line on the sides of the neck. Underparts whitish. Forest in central and eastern H (and foothills in N) and NE.

PITTAS Pittidae. 5 species. P. 78. Only the Indian Pitta occurs widely; 3 species are found only in eastern H and NE. **Hooded Pitta** *Pitta sordida*. 20cm. Head and neck black; green above and below, red under tail. Blue on rump and wings. H (and foothills) and NE.

LARKS Alaudidae. 20 species. P. 78. A confusing family in the field; several species can only be identified satisfactorily in the hand. **Rufous-winged Bushlark** *Mirafra assamica.* 15cm. Like Red-winged, but darker and greyer; somewhat heavier build. Chestnut in wings less obvious. N, NE, P, Sri Lanka. **Singing Bushlark** *M. javanica.* 15cm. Very similar, but can be told in field by white outer tail feathers. NW, N, NE, H, P. **Black-crowned Finchlark** *Eremopterix nigriceps.* 13cm. Both sexes paler sandy than Ashycrowned. Male has white forehead and cheeks, black crown, throat and underparts. NW. **Rufous-tailed Finchlark** *Ammomanes phoenicurus.* 16cm. Rufous-brown, with broad black tip to rufous tail. Dry, open country in NW, N, P. **Malabar Crested Lark** *Galerida malabarica.* 15cm. Like Crested, but rich brown on back, streaked darker. Throat and belly whitish, heavy brown streaking on breast. Open country in western P. **Deccan Crested Lark** *G. deva.* 13cm. Like smaller Malabar, but underparts more uniform and darker orange-buff. NW, N, and P.

SWALLOWS and **MARTINS** Hirundinidae. 13 species. P. 80. **Plain Sand Martin** *Riparia paludicola* 12cm. Light uniform greyish-brown above; paler below with whitish belly. Wings and tail darker brown. Open country with sandy cliffs or river-banks in NW, N, NE, and northern P. **Crag Martin** *Hirundo rupestris.* 14cm. Like Dusky Crag Martin but paler brown above and whitish below, with dark patch in 'armpit'. White spots show on fanned tail. Breeds H, wintering to hills in P. **House Swallow** *H. tahitica.* 13cm. Like Common Swallow, but tail streamers short; lacks blue breast band. Common in SW and Sri Lanka. **House Martin** *Delichon urbica.* 15cm. Black above, glossy on head and back, with contrasting white rump. White below. Tail noticeably forked. Race in most of H has white parts markedly off-white. H, wintering to NE and southern P. **Nepal House Martin** *D. nipalensis.* 14cm. Like House Martin but tail square-ended, not forked, and chin and undertail coverts black, quite easily seen from below. H, NE to foothills in winter.

PIPITS and **WAGTAILS** Motacillidae. 18 species. P. 82. The 12 species of Pipits are confusing in the field – important points include degree of streaking, call and leg-length. **Indian Tree Pipit** *Anthus hodgsoni.* 15cm. Greenish-brown above with obscure streaking, and well-marked heavy streaks on breast and flanks. Whitish eye-stripe, dark stripe through eye. Loud wheezy 'tseep' call. Wags tail and perches in trees. Breeds commonly in H, wintering widely to southern P; not in NW or Sri Lanka. **Tree Pipit** *A. trivialis.* 15cm. Clear buffy brown above with dark streaking, and pale yellowy-buff below with fine dark streaking on breast. Winters in open country throughout area except Sri Lanka.

Tawny Pipit *A. campestris.* 15cm. Slim, long-legged and pale. Light brown above, hardly streaked, but conspicuous dark centres to median wing-coverts. Buffy breast with streaking absent or very faint. Widespread in winter; not in Sri Lanka. **Brown Rock Pipit** *A. similis.* 20cm. Large size and long bill noticeable. Rather uniform brownish, paler and buffier below. Indistinct smudgy streaks above, faint streaking on breast. Breeds NW and SW; in winter in dry or cultivated country in N, NE and northern P as well. **Nilgiri Pipit** *A. nilghiriensis.* 17cm. Like a dark Indian Pipit, with dark streaking on breast and flanks more extensive. Confined to hills in SW. **Grey Wagtail** *Motacilla cinerea.* 17cm. Long tail. Blue-grey above. Breeding male has black throat and bright yellow underparts. Female and winter male duller above, throat whitish, yellow on belly and vent. Rump always greeny-yellow. Outer tail feathers white. Common breeder by streams in H, wintering south throughout area.

CUCKOO-SHRIKES and **MINIVETS** Campephagidae. 16 species. P. 84. **Pied Flycatcher-Shrike** *Hemipus picatus.* 14cm. Behaviour like flycatcher. Head and upperparts black. White collar, rump, underparts, bar on wing, and tail edges. Female browner. Forests in H, NE, P, and Sri Lanka. **White-bellied Minivet** *Pericrocotus erythropygius.* 15cm. Head, back and wings black. Breast and rump orange. White underparts and wing-patch. Female browner. Open forests in P, except extreme south and east.

BULBULS Pycnonotidae. 20 species. P. 86. **Black-crested Yellow Bulbul** *Pycnonotus melanicterus.* 18cm. Black head and throat. Yellow-green above, bright yellow underparts. In H, NE and parts of north-central and north-eastern P has black pointed crest. In SW uncrested and throat red. In Sri Lanka uncrested and throat black. **Yellow-eared Bulbul** *P. penicillatus.* 20cm. No crest. Green above, underparts yellow. Crown brown; white line over eye, and tuft of yellow feathers behind eye. Hill woodland, confined to Sri Lanka. **Yellow-browed Bulbul** *Hypsipetes indicus.* 20cm. No crest. Yellow forehead and line over eye. Olive above, with yellow underparts. Forests in western P and Sri Lanka. **Brown-eared Bulbul** *H. flavala.* 20cm. Short crest. Brownish wings with large yellow patch. Dark head with light brown ear-coverts. Darkish grey above, underparts whitish. H, foothills in N, and NE, in woodland.

IORAS, LEAFBIRDS, FAIRY BLUEBIRD Irenidae. 6 species. P. 88. **Orange-bellied Leafbird** *Chloropsis hardwickii.* 19cm. Wings and tail blue-black. Throat and sides of face black, underparts orange. Crown and back green. Female paler, with no black on throat or tail. Woodland in H and NE.

WAXWINGS Bombycillidae. 1 species. **Waxwing** *Bombycilla garrulus.* 18cm. A pinkish-grey crested arboreal bird. Black chin. Tail tipped yellow. Irregular in winter in H.

HYPOCOLIUS Hypocoliidae. 1 species. **Grey Hypocolius** *Hypocolius ampelinus.* 25cm. A grey, shrike-like bird. Black primaries with broad white tips. Black eye-stripe. Irregular in dry scrub in open country or sub-desert in NW.

DIPPERS Cinclidae. 2 species. **Brown Dipper** *Cinclus pallasii.* 20cm. Like a short-tailed dumpy thrush. All dark brown. Cocks tail and bobs when at rest. On rocks in hill streams in H and NE.

WRENS Troglodytidae. 1 species. **Wren** *Troglodytes troglodytes.* 9cm. Tiny; cocks short tail. Dark rufous-brown, paler below, with darker cross-barring. Rattling alarm note. Common in undergrowth or rocky places in H.

ACCENTORS Prunellidae. 8 species. **Rufous-breasted Accentor** *Prunella strophiata.* 15cm. Dark rich brown above with darker streaks. Two pale wing-bars. Whitish throat contrasts with rufous breast; belly whitish, streaky. Pale rusty supercilium contrasts with dark cheeks. Unobtrusive; hops about on ground in pairs or small groups; flicks wings. H. **Blackthroated Accentor** *P. atrogularis.* 15cm. Dark crown, cheeks and throat. Buff below with dark streaks on flanks. Buff supercilium. Streaky brown above with two pale wing-bars. In winter in NW and western H. The other 6 species are all high altitude breeders in H.

THRUSHES, ROBINS, CHATS and **FORKTAILS** Turdidae. 89 species. P. 94–6. **Indian Blue Chat** *Erithacus brunneus.* 15cm. Shape much as Black Redstart. Blue above with short white stripe over eye. Sides of head black. Bright rufous below, whitish on belly. Female brown, paler below. Breeds H, wintering to NE, SW and Sri Lanka. **Redflanked Bush-Robin** *E. cyanurus.* 15cm. Male has upperparts and sides of head dark blue. Forehead, rump and shoulders bright blue. Flanks orange, centre of throat to belly white. Female similar but paler; light brown above, bluer on rump and tail. Lacks dark sides of head and throat. Flanks orange. Undergrowth in H and NE. **Dark Grey Bush-Chat** *Saxicola ferrea.* 15cm. Like Pied Bush-Chat, but underparts and a conspicuous supercilium white. Breast grey, and upperparts greyish-brown streaked darker. Female rufous-brown, paler eyestripe and underparts, throat white. H and NE, in winter to N. **Isabelline Wheatear** *Oenanthe isabellina.* 16cm. Mainly sandy-brown, paler below and darker on wings. Conspicuous white tail with broad black tip. Stands upright or runs about actively on open ground. Arid plains in NW. **Pied Wheatear** *O. picata.* 15cm. Male is either all-black with white rump and base of tail, or with crown and belly white as well. Female similar but dark brown instead of black. Arid areas of NW. **River Chat** *Chaimarrornis leucocephalus.* 19cm. Crown white; rest of head, breast and upperparts black. Underparts, rump and tail chestnut, tail with black tip. Rocky streams in H. **Blue-headed Rock Thrush** *Monticola cinclorhynchus.* 18cm. Male has crown, shoulders and throat blue. Sides of face, back and tail black, with white wing-patch. Rump and underparts rufous. Female brown above, paler below with dark scaly pattern. Breeds in H, wintering through western P. **Malabar Whistling Thrush** *Myiophoneus horsfieldii.* 25cm. Blackish-blue above and below, with bright blue on forehead and shoulder. Bill black. Whistling song. Streams in hill jungle in western P. There is a similar species, *M. blighi*, in Sri Lanka. **Orange-headed Ground Thrush** *Zoothera citrina.* 22cm. Blue-grey back, white wing patch. Orange head and underparts. Peninsular race has black and white cheek pattern. Forests in H, NE and P. **White's Thrush** *Z. dauma.* 25cm. Yellowish-brown, whiter on underparts. Bold black and buff scaling on back, and black crescent-shaped marks on face, sides of breast and flanks. Black and white band on underwing. Forest undergrowth in H, NE, SW and Sri Lanka. **Spotted-winged Ground Thrush** *Z. spiloptera.* 21cm. White underparts with bold dark spotting. Brown above with noticeable white tips to wing coverts. Restricted to Sri Lanka, mostly in hill woodland. **Plain-backed Mountain Thrush** *Z. mollissima.* 27cm. Uniform brown upperparts and buffy, heavily spotted underparts. A similar species, *Z. dixoni*, has two pale wing-bars. Open or scrubby hillsides in H.

Tickell's Thrush *Turdus unicolor.* 22cm. Uniform ashy plumage, paler on underparts. Underwing rufous. Woodland. Breeds H, winters to NW, N, and NE. **White-collared Blackbird** *T. albocinctus.* 27cm. White collar and throat, otherwise blackish. Bill yellow. Common in H. **Grey-winged Blackbird** *T. boulboul.* 28cm. Black above and below with large pale grey wing-patch. Bill orange. Female browner. Forests in H and NE. **Black-throated Thrush** *T. ruficollis.* 25cm. Brownish-grey above. Underparts white; black throat and breast in summer, mottled with whitish fringes in winter. Female browner. H, NE, N, and NW in winter. **Little Forktail** *Enicurus scouleri.* 12cm. Wagtail-like. Black head and throat, upperparts, wings and tail. White forehead, underparts, wing-bar, rump and tail edges. Tail slightly forked, and is constantly wagged, and also expanded and shut. Legs white. Hill streams in H and NE. **Spotted Forktail** *E. maculatus.* 25cm. Similar but much larger, with very long deeply forked tail. Upperparts black with white spots and wing-bar; forehead and underparts white. Tail black with white tips and edges. Legs pinky-white. By hill streams in woodland in H and NE.

WARBLERS Sylviidae. 91 species. P. 98. The identification of a number of the warblers in the field is often very difficult; with some it is necessary to have the bird in the hand. However, with practice a good many can be distinguished; it helps to keep careful notes of voice as well as plumage, actions and habitat. For a comprehensive treatment see Volume 8 of The Handbook. Only a very small selection of more readily identified species can be described here. **Redheaded Fantail** *Cisticola exilis.* 10cm. Very like Streaked Fantail but when breeding has crown unstreaked bright orangey-gold. Tail longer, and tipped buff not white. In winter best mark is gingery collar. Common in southern P, and NE. **Grey-breasted Prinia** *Prinia hodgsonii.* 12cm. Like Ashy Prinia, but whiter underparts with grey breast-band. Browner in winter, when more northern races lose the grey breast. Common in bushes and scrub in H, N, NE, P, and Sri Lanka.

Rufous-fronted Prinia *P. buchanani.* 12cm. Like Indian Prinia but darker, and forehead and crown rufous. Whitish below and greyish-brown above. Low scrub in dry, open country in NW, western parts of N, and north and west P. **Jungle Prinia** *P. sylvatica.* 15cm. Like Indian Prinia but darker; dull brown above, more rufous on rump. Pale buff round and over eye. Underparts all pale buff. Common in grass and scrub in N, NE, P, and Sri Lanka.

Clamorous Warbler *Acrocephalus stentoreus.* 19cm. A large, unstreaked warbler; olive-brown above and buffy white below, with white throat and supercilium. Loud harsh repetitive song. Reedbeds or waterside vegetation. Breeds NW and NE; widespread, to Sri Lanka, in winter.

Blyth's Reed Warbler *A. dumetorum.* 15cm. Similar to Clamorous Warbler, but smaller; pale buffy supercilium very noticeable. Rounded tailtip. Common in bushes and scrub in winter throughout the area.

Booted Warbler *Hippolais caligata.* 12cm. Pale greyish-brown above, buffy-white below. Pale patch in front of eye. Tail square-ended, often flicked. Flycatches from foliage. Winters throughout area south of H, common in NW, in bushes and scrub. **Leaf Warblers.** The Brown Chiffchaff is typical of this large and confusing group of 20 species – some winter visitors, many breeding in the Himalayas.

Tickell's Leaf Warbler *Phylloscopus affinis.* 12cm. Dark olive above. Underparts and long supercilium bright yellow. Common breeder in high H, wintering widely to southern P. **Yellow-browed Leaf Warbler** *P. inornatus.* 11cm. Greyish-green above, with two pale wing bars. Whitish below. Long pale supercilium. Common breeder H, wintering widely to southern P. **Crowned Leaf Warbler** *P. occipitalis.* 12cm. Light yellowish-olive above, 2 (only one well-marked) wing-bars. Whitish below. Yellow supercilium and dark eye-stripe. Common breeder in western H, wintering widely to P.

FLYCATCHERS Muscicapidae. 35 species. P. 92. **Ultramarine Flycatcher** *Ficedula superciliaris.* 10cm. Upperparts, sides of head and neck deep blue. White stripe above eye and white sides to base of tail in western H birds. Centre of throat to belly white. Female paler and browner. Breeds H and NE, wintering to central P. **Black and Orange Flycatcher** *F. nigrorufa.* 13cm. Black head and wings, rest of plumage bright rufous. Sexes alike. Undergrowth in hill forests in SW.

Rufous-bellied Niltava *Niltava sundara.* 15cm. Throat and upperparts deep blue-black. Glossy blue patch on side of neck. Crown, rump and shoulders bright blue. Underparts orange. Female brown, rufous on tail, with blue neck patch. Undergrowth in H and NE.

Dusky Blue Flycatcher *Muscicapa sordida.* 14cm. All blue-grey, brighter on forehead. Black patch in front of eye. Belly whitish. Sexes alike. Undergrowth in hill forests in Sri Lanka. **Verditer Flycatcher** *M. thalassina.* 15cm. All blue-green with black patch in front of eye. Wings and tail darker. Female duller. Common breeder in H, wintering throughout area except NW and Sri Lanka.

FANTAIL FLYCATCHERS Rhipiduridae. 3 species. P. 92. **Yellow-bellied Fantail** *Rhipidura hypoxantha.* 11cm. Shape as in other fantails. Dark grey above with forehead and eyestripe yellow. Sides of head black. Underparts yellow. Forests in H and NE.

PARADISE FLYCATCHERS Monarchidae. 2 species. P. 92. **Black-naped Monarch** *Monarcha azurea.* 15cm. Long tail. Mainly rich blue but belly white. Black patch on back of head and across breast. Female browner without black patches. Flits rather like Fantails. Woodland in N, NE and P to Sri Lanka.

WHISTLERS Pachycephalidae. 1 species. **Mangrove Whistler** *Pachycephala grisola.* 16cm. Like a thick-set warbler. Grey-brown above, paler below. Has a rising whistle, repeated several times. Coastal mangroves in NE.

BABBLERS Timaliidae. 125 species. Pp. 100–104. Only a small selection of relatively common or easily identified species can be dealt with here. For a comprehensive and detailed treatment see The Handbook. **Brown-capped Babbler** *Pellorneum fuscocapillum.* 16cm. Shape as Spotted Babbler. Brown above with a darker cap. Eyestripe, face and underparts cinnamon-buff. Confined to Sri Lanka; common. **Red-capped Babbler** *Timalia pileata.* 17cm. Shape much as Spotted Babbler. Bill stout, black. Crown bright chestnut; supercilium, sides of face, throat and breast white. Upperparts olive. Belly and flanks buffy. Undergrowth and grass in N, NE, north-eastern P and Mysore. **White-headed Babbler** *Turdoides affinis.* 23cm. Shape as in Jungle Babbler. Bill and feet yellow. Pale buffy-white crown contrasts with dark brownish ear-coverts. Brown above and below, the throat and breast darker and more scaly than in Jungle Babbler. Scrub, gardens. P and Sri Lanka. **Ceylon Rufous Babbler** *T. rufescens.* 25cm. Shape as in Jungle Babbler. Ginger brown with cinnamon throat and breast, head greyer. Orange bill and legs. Noisy. Forests. Confined to Sri Lanka. **Ashy-headed Laughing Thrush** *Garrulax cinereifrons.* 23cm. Shape as in White-throated L-T. Head grey, throat whitish. Dark, rich brown above, underparts pale cinnamon. Bill black. Forests in Sri Lanka.

Black-gorgeted Laughing Thrush *G. pectoralis.* 29cm. Brown above, with white-tipped tail. A conspicuous black line through eyes encircles breast, bordered on inside with broad white line; throat more buffy. Belly white, flanks buffy. There is a similar, slightly smaller species, *G. moniliger*, with throat white, and necklace narrower or incomplete. H, NE. **Rufous-vented Laughing Thrush** *G. delesserti.* 23cm. Brown above, crown greyer. Belly and vent chestnut. In SW, throat white shading to greyish breast. In NE, throat and breast yellow. Hill forests. **Kerala Laughing Thrush** *G. jerdoni.* 20cm. Throat and breast grey, belly rufous. Upperparts brownish, with white stripe over eye. Scrub in SW. **Red-headed Laughing Thrush** *G. erythrocephalus.* 28cm. Crown and nape rufous; olive-brown upperparts with yellowish wings. Throat and scaling on breast and back blackish. Looks dark in field. Undergrowth. H, NE.

Silver-eared Mesia *Leiothrix argentauris.* 15cm. Shape much as Pekin Robin, but tail square-ended. Black crown, ear coverts silvery. Greeny-grey back, with red and yellow in wing. Breast and bill orange. Light woodland in H, NE.

Stripe-throated Yuhina *Yuhina gularis.* 14cm. Shape as in Yellow-naped Yuhina. Brown above with orange streak in wing. Underparts paler, with dark streaking on throat. Woodland. H, NE.

White-browed Tit-Babbler *Alcippe vinipectus.* 11cm. Shape as in Chestnut-headed Tit-Babbler. Broad white eye-stripe. Crown, ear-coverts and back dark, rich brown. Underparts whitish, duskier on belly. Forests in H, NE.

LONGTAILED TITS Aegithalidae. 4 species. P. 106.

TITS Paridae. 13 species. P. 106. **Green-backed Tit** *Parus monticolus.* 13cm. Pattern as in Grey Tit, but back green and underparts yellow. NE; common in H, to foothills in N in winter. **Black Tit** *P. rubidiventris.* 13cm. Crested head and breast black, cheeks and nape white. Upperparts grey. Belly, flanks and under-tail coverts rufous in central H; belly grey in western H. High altitude woodland in H.

NUTHATCHES Sittidae. 7 species. P. 106.

WALL-CREEPER Tichodromadidae. 1 species.

TREE-CREEPERS Certhiidae. 5 species. P. 106.

PENDULINE TITS Remizidae. 2 species.

SUNBIRDS and **SPIDERHUNTERS** Nectariniidae. 14 species. P. 108.

Rubycheek *Anthreptes singalensis.* 10cm. Short straight bill. Shining green above. Ear coverts coppery. Throat and breast rufous, rest of underparts yellow. Female dull olive above; like pale male below. NE. **Maroon-breasted Sunbird** *Nectarinia lotenia.* 13cm. Like Purple Sunbird, but bill longer and more curved. Dark crimson breast band. Female olive above, yellow below. Southern P. and Sri Lanka. **Mrs Gould's Sunbird** *Aethopyga gouldiae.* 15cm. Scarlet back, purple crown and throat. Underparts and rump yellow. Tail bright blue. Female dull green with short tail and yellow rump. Forests in H and NE. **Green-tailed Sunbird** *A. nipalensis.* 15cm. Greeny-black head and throat. Upper back dark maroon, wings dark brown. Rump and underparts bright yellow, tail green. Female dull olive, paler below. Forests in H and NE. **Fire-tailed Sunbird** *A. ignicauda.* 15cm. Face, crown and throat purple-black. Back and long tail scarlet; rump and underparts yellow. Female dull olive. Forests in H and NE. **Little Spiderhunter** *Arachnothera longirostris.* 14cm. Like a large female sunbird with long, curved bill. Dark olive above; throat whitish. Belly and flanks yellowish. Forests in eastern H, NE and SW.

FLOWERPECKERS Dicaeidae. 9 species. P. 108. **Scarlet-backed Flowerpecker** *Dicaeum cruentatum.* 7cm. Black sides of face and breast; black wings and tail. Scarlet band from forehead to rump. Underparts pale buffy. Female brown above, red only above tail. Common in NE. **Fire-breasted Flowerpecker** *D. ignipectus.* 7cm. Dark oily green head and upperparts; bright buff below, with scarlet splash on breast, and black streak below it. Common in woods in H.

WHITE-EYES Zosteropidae. 2 species. P. 108.

ORIOLES Oriolidae. 4 species. P. 120. **Maroon Oriole** *Oriolus traillii.* 28cm. Head and wings black; rest of plumage maroon, tail brighter and lighter. Forests in H, NE.

SHRIKES Laniidae. 9 species. P. 90.

DRONGOS Dicruridae. 9 species. P. 122. **Grey Drongo** *Dicrurus leucophaeus.* 30cm. Like Common Drongo, but underparts dull grey. Keeps more to wooded areas. Breeds H and NE. Widespread in winter as far as Sri Lanka. **Bronzed Drongo** *D. aeneus.* 24cm. Small; shallow tail fork. Plumage highly glossed. Glades in woodland in H, N, NE, and eastern and western P. **Spangled Drongo** *D. hottentotus.* 31cm. Very glossy. Shallow fork in tail, but tips markedly up-curved. Bill pointed and down-curved. Noisy. Forests in H, N, NE, and parts of western and north-eastern P.

SWALLOW-SHRIKES Artamidae. 2 species. P. 90.

JAYS, MAGPIES, TREEPIES and **CROWS** Corvidae. 22 species. P. 122. **Black-throated Jay** *Garrulus lanceolatus.* 33cm. Black head and neck, streaked white on throat. Wings and tail black with blue barring, rest of plumage pinky-grey. White patch on wing in flight. Light woodland in western and central H. **Green Magpie** *Cissa chinensis.* 38cm. Bright green plumage with rufous wings. Black eye-stripe. Long tail tipped black and white. Red bill and legs. Noisy. Himalayan foothills in N and NE in thick forest. **Ceylon Blue Magpie** *C. ornata.* 47cm. Bill and legs red. Chestnut head, breast, back and wings. Rest of plumage bright blue, the long tail tipped black and white. Forest, confined to Sri Lanka. **Himalayan Tree-Pie** *Dendrocitta formosae.* 40cm. Forehead, chin and throat blackish, nape and upper back grey. Lower back brown. Browny-grey below, chestnut under tail. Wings black, with white patch in flight. H, N and NE. **White-bellied Tree-Pie** *D. leucogastra.* 50cm. Face and breast black. Back of head, neck and underparts white. Chestnut back. Wings black with white patch. Forest in SW. **Jackdaw** *Corvus monedula.* 33cm. Small black crow with stumpy beak. Back of head grey, eyes white. In cultivated land, gregarious. Common breeder in Kashmir, dispersing in winter in NW. **Raven** *C. corax.* 70cm. Like large Jungle Crow. Massive bill; loose, pointed throat feathers. Wedge-shaped tail best seen in flight. Deep croak. NW, N and H.

STARLINGS, MYNAS and **GRACKLES** Sturnidae. 19 species. Pp. 116, 118. **Ceylon Hill Myna** *Gracula ptilogenys.* 25cm. Like Hill Myna, but only has two small yellow wattles at rear of crown. Woodland. Confined to Sri Lanka.

SPARROWS and **SNOW-FINCHES** Passeridae. 13 species. P. 114. **Tree Sparrow** *Passer montanus.* 15cm. Like male House Sparrow, but crown rich brown, and a black patch on white cheeks. Sexes alike. Often around houses. NW, H, and NE. **Cinnamon Tree Sparrow** *P. rutilans.* 15cm. Bright rufous cap and upperparts. Cheeks and underparts pale yellow. Small black chin patch. Female rich buff with pale eye-stripe. Wood-edge or cultivation in H.

WEAVERS Ploceidae. 4 species. P. 114.

MUNIAS Estrildidae. 8 species. P. 112.

FINCHES Fringillidae. 42 species. P. 110. **Black and Yellow Grosbeak** *Mycerobas icterioides.* 22cm. Huge conical bill. Black head and breast, wings and tail. Underparts, collar and centre of back yellow. Female grey-brown, buffy below. Forests in western H. There are 3 rather similar species. **Himalayan Goldfinch** *Carduelis carduelis.* 14cm. Scarlet face. Pale brown above, wings black with golden band.

Tail black with white tip. Open country or light woodland in western H. There are 14 species of **Rosefinches** Carpodacus in the Himalayas, mostly breeding at high altitudes. For details refer to the Handbook. **Orange Bullfinch** *Pyrrhula aurantiaca.* 14cm. Face, wings and tail black, the wings with a broad pale bar. Rump white. Remainder of plumage golden-buff. Female greyer on back, head and neck. Undergrowth, woods, in western H.

BUNTINGS Emberizidae. 16 species. P. 110. **Yellow-breasted Bunting** *Emberiza aureola.* 15cm. Black face and cheeks. Chestnut hind crown, back, and band across chest. White shoulder patch. Underparts yellow. Female streaky brown above, yellower below. Common in winter on cultivated ground in NE. **Black-faced Bunting** *E. spodocephala.* 15cm. Olive-green head, neck and breast; black around base of bill. Underparts pale yellow. Back streaky brown, rump greenish. Female streaky brown, yellower on belly. Common in scrub and cultivation in winter in NE. **White-capped Bunting** *E. stewarti.* 15cm. Back and breastband light chestnut. Head light grey with broad black eyestripe and black patch on chin and throat. Female streaky brown, rufous on rump. Pale buffy below, streaked on breast. Open hillsides in western H and NW, in winter to N. **Crested Bunting** *Melophus lathami.* 15cm. Male has erect crest. Wings and tail dark chestnut, rest of plumage black. Female duller with shorter crest. Open country in NW, H, N and NE.

Topography of a Bird

Although it is not the function of this book to supply highly technical or detailed plumage descriptions, it is important to know the correct names for the exterior parts and feathering of a bird. Use of these terms leads to sharper and more knowledgeable field observation, and is essential for making accurate notes about a bird you have seen or handled.

Because of the great differences in shape and proportions, especially the shape of the folded wing, between the different families of birds, the feather groups do not always appear as neatly grouped and distinct as in the bunting drawn opposite. In many large birds such as vultures, the secondaries completely overlap the primaries in the closed wing, while in game-birds the upper-tail coverts may reach to the end of the central tail feathers. Certain groups of feathers often become modified in shape, and attention is drawn to some of these variations below.

1 Bill, consisting of an upper and a lower mandible. The nostrils in the upper mandible may be exposed, or covered by feathers or bristles. Birds such as barbets and flycatchers have stiff bristles around the gape and base of the bill known as rictal bristles. **2** Forehead, often distinctively coloured. **3** Eye. The coloured part around the black pupil is the iris. Many birds have an eye-ring, a narrow ring of feathers, often white, and sometimes incomplete. Note that the eyelids in some birds, eg doves, may be swollen or brightly coloured. **4** Supercilium. A streak above the eye, normally pale. A line through the eye, usually dark, is best referred to as an eye-stripe. **5** Crown. The feathers are sometimes elongated to form a crest. **6** Ear coverts. **7** Nape. **8** Chin. **9** Throat. **10** Breast. **11** Flanks, sometimes concealed under the closed wing-edge in small birds, but in game-birds overlaps the wing-edge and may be conspicuously patterned. **12** Belly. **13** Under-tail coverts. Usually lie flat under the base of the tail. **14** Mantle. **15** Back. **16** Rump. **17** Upper-tail coverts. **18** Tail. **19** Lesser wing-coverts. **20** Median wing-coverts. Sometimes have paler tips, forming a wing-bar, and often have dark centres. They overlap the opposite way from, and overlie the bases of the next group of feathers. **21** Greater wing-coverts. These also often have paler or contrastingly coloured tips. **22** Primary coverts, often more conspicuous on the open than the closed wing. They overlie the bases of the primaries. **23** Secondaries. The feathers which form the rear margin of the open wing, and with the primaries are referred to as the flight feathers. The inner ones are sometimes elongated, as in ducks and shorebirds, and are referred to as tertiaries. In ducks the secondaries are often brightly coloured with

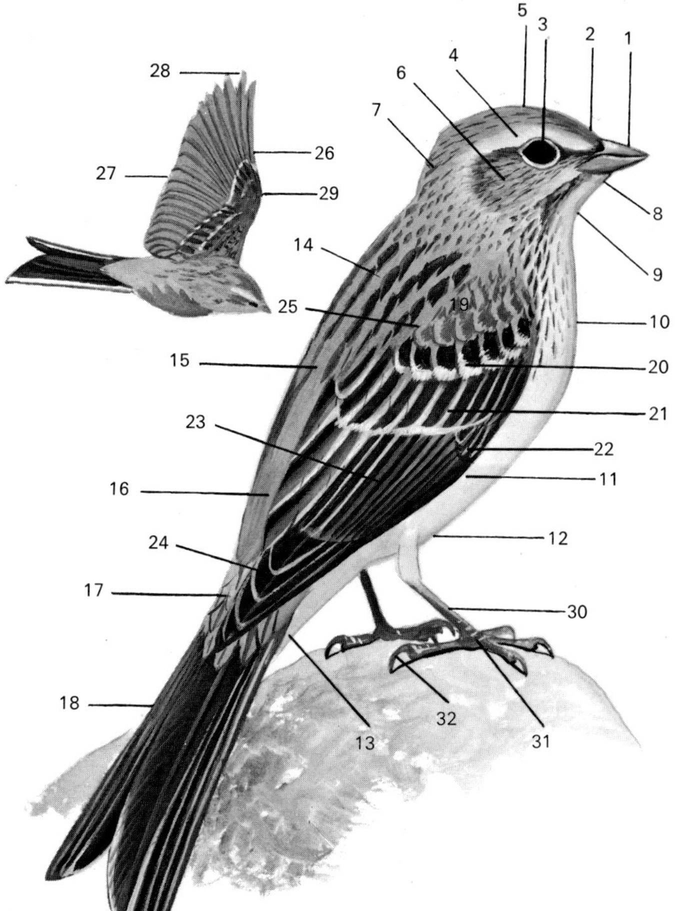

iridescent colours and contrasting tips or bases. This patch of colour and pattern is called the speculum. **24** Primaries. Their relative lengths determine the shape of the wing-tip. **25** Scapulars. Feathers covering the shoulder, often distinctively patterned. **26** and **27** Leading and trailing edges of wing. **28** Wing-tip. **29** Bend of wing. On the underwing, the coverts are usually referred to as the wing lining. The axillaries are a group of feathers lying in the 'armpit' between the wing lining and the flank. **30** Tarsus, often referred to loosely as the leg. Above it is the thigh or shank. **31** Foot, consisting in most birds of 4 toes. Normally the first toe points backwards, but swifts have all toes pointing forward, and cuckoos, woodpeckers and parrots have two pointing forward and two back. The toes are sometimes joined by webs. **32** Claw.

Glossary

A brief explanation of some terms which are either used in this book, or may occur in other works on the natural history of India.

Adult Term used to indicate a bird which has attained the final plumage of its species. Although it may moult into seasonal plumages these are stable and do not change with age. Note that many birds breed before assuming adult plumage.

Affinity Denotes a family relationship or common ancestor. It is usually indicated by a structural or behavioural resemblance.

Allopatric Related species whose breeding ranges do not overlap.

Altricial Nestlings which are helpless and naked on hatching, requiring brooding and feeding. Songbird nestlings are typical.

Arboreal Tree-frequenting.

Avian Pertaining to birds. (Latin *Avis*: a bird)

Avifauna The various bird species of a particular area.

Banyan The wild fig-tree *Ficus benghalensis*

Bhabar Belt of rich loamy soil north of the *Terai*. Extends up to about 600m. in the Himalayan foothills; supports tall forest.

Binomial Refers in nomenclature to a designation consisting of a generic and a specific name only. Also called binominal.

Biome A stable community of animals and plants making up a well-defined "life-zone" or "biotic community" such as tropical scrub forest, broad-leaved evergreen forest, desert, etc.

Biotope A location where a community of any given type exists.

Bund An artificial embankment or causeway.

Casque The horn-like outgrowth above the bill of most Hornbills.

Congeneric Refers to species of the same genus.

Conspecific Refers to individuals of the same species.

Contour feathers Outer feathers with well-defined webs or vanes (as opposed to down), on body, wings and tail.

Crepuscular Active at twilight.

Dimorphic Having two forms (as in the plumage phases of the Collared Scops Owl).

Diurnal Active in the daytime.

Duars The parts of the *Bhabar* east of about Darjeeling.

Duns Broad valleys in the outer Himalayas and Siwaliks.

Eclipse A plumage worn by males of certain species (ducks, some sunbirds) after the breeding season.

Ecotone Area where two biotopes overlap or blend ("Edge effect").

Endemic Confined to a certain area (Indigenous).

Family A group of related genera; an important taxonomic unit.

Feral Domesticated animal or bird living wild after escaping.

Fledge A stage at which a chick can flutter from the nest or off the ground – ie, it implies a specific stage of feather growth.

Form A less exact term than race or sub-species, it refers to a recognizable grouping which may be taxonomic or not, eg colour phases.

Genus A taxonomic grouping of closely related species. (Plural *Genera*).

Ghats In its primary sense a passage or steps leading down to a river or ford. Applied to the steep-sided, flat-topped hills which run parallel to the east and west coasts of the Peninsular. (Ghauts).

Hawking Catching insects in the air with bill or foot.

Immature A fully grown bird which has not assumed adult plumage. A stage which may last 2 to 4 years in large birds.

Jheel A shallow lake or intermittently flooded wetland with both submerged and emergent vegetation.

Juvenile A bird in its first complete contour feathering.

Nidification Relating to nests and nesting habits.

Nocturnal Active at night.

Nullah A stream bed or watercourse.

Oology The study of eggs, especially their exterior and markings.

Paddyfield Ricefield.

Passerine A species in the Order Passeriformes – the perching or song-birds. (All the families from Broadbills and Pittas onward in this book.)

Phase A constant plumage variation not related to age or sex.

Pipal A wild fig-tree *Ficus religiosa*.

Precocial Nestlings which are active and feathered on hatching.

Shola A patch of forest, usually in a small valley, surrounded by grassland or crops.

Siwaliks The low outermost hills of the Himalayas, extending along the entire southern border of the range. Composed of washed-down debris which was then compressed, folded and elevated. Famous for the richness of the fossil fauna.

Species/Subspecies See Introduction, page 7.

Sympatric Related species with overlapping breeding ranges.

Synonym Refers to names where more than one has been given to any single taxonomic category.

Tank A large artificial lake or reservoir.

Taxonomy The classification of organisms according to their relationships.

Terai The strip of alluvial land between the *Bhabar* and the north Indian plains. Often marshy, or with tall grass or scattered patches of forest.

Terrestrial Ground-frequenting.

Trinomial A scientific name in three parts – generic, specific, and sub-specific. Also called trinominal.

Zygodactyle Having two toes pointing forwards and two back, as in cuckoos and woodpeckers.

Bibliography

This book is designed primarily as a simple introduction to Indian birds in the field, but hopefully it will stimulate the kind of continuous and developing interest in bird study for which more advanced books, and wider reading generally, are a happy necessity. There is a rich treasure-house of literature to plunder, and the following annotated list, arranged under six headings, covers a range of titles to cater for every taste and need. Some are luxuries, and some necessities, but all are books the present writer has found useful or interesting. Those believed to be still in print are marked with a star; many of the others are available from time to time from dealers in second-hand books.

Bird books for general reference;
basic texts covering the whole field of bird-life.

Austin, O.L. *Birds of the World** Hamlyn, London. A comprehensive survey with abundant colour illustrations.

Farner, D.S. & J.R. King *Avian Biology* 5 vols.* Academic Press New York. An advanced scientific reference work.

Fisher, J. & R.T. Peterson *The World of Birds* London 1964.

Thomson, A.L. (Ed.) *A New Dictionary of Birds* London 1964. An indispensable one-volume encyclopaedia.

van Tyne, J. & A.J. Berger *Fundamentals of Ornithology** 2nd Ed. John Wiley, New York and London. One of the best single volumes; has a detailed description of all the bird families, one page per family.

Welty, J.C. *The Life of Birds** 2nd Ed. W.B. Saunders & Co. Philadelphia. Another excellent single volume treatise.

Textbooks or guides to Indian Birds.

Ali, Salim *The Book of Indian Birds** Revised and expanded edition 1972. A popular pocket guide dealing with the commoner birds, which has gone into nine editions since it first appeared in 1941.
*Indian Hill Birds** A delightfully written pocket guide, but does not cover all the Himalayan species.
& S. Dillon Ripley *Handbook of the Birds of India and Pakistan* 10 vols.* 1968–74. The definitive work. An absolute necessity for the student of Indian birds; a second, revised, edition is currently appearing; volumes 1, 2 and 3 have now been published. Covers all bird species in the sub-continent in great detail, with many maps, line drawings and colour plates.

Baker, E.C. Stuart *Fauna of British India – Birds.* 8 vols. 1922–1930. The second edition of the bird volumes in this series. Still of value for the detailed plumage descriptions (to which the reader of the *Handbook* is referred,) though out-of-date on scientific names and range. It has been described by one authority, not uncontroversial himself, as "a compendium of ornithological inexactitudes."

Jerdon, T.C. *The Birds of India* 3 vols. 1862–64. The first, and a very good, attempt at a comprehensive avifauna, by one of the leading authorities of the last century (a period when India boasted many of the finest field ornithologists in the world). Still very readable, with much worthwhile information on habits.

Oates, E.W. & W.T. Blanford *Fauna of British India – Birds* 4 vols. 1889-98. The bird volumes in a multi-volume treatise on Indian natural history. Baker owed much to the descriptions and nice line drawings, mostly of heads, which he used in his edition.

Ripley, S. Dillon *A Synopsis of the Birds of India and Pakistan* 1961. A comprehensive faunal list with data on range and status, precursor to the *Handbook*. A new edition is in preparation.

Whistler, Hugh *The Popular Handbook of Indian Birds* 4th Ed. 1949. A well-written but by no means comprehensive guide by a first-class field ornithologist.

Regional reference works and guides.

Ali, Salim *Field Guide to the Birds of the Eastern Himalayas** Oxford University Press 1977. A first-class field guide, with 37 coloured plates, some reproduced from the *Birds of Sikkim*.

Birds of Kerala 1969. An essential reference work to the birds of south-west India.

The Birds of Kutch 1945

The Birds of Sikkim 1962. With 17 excellent colour plates of many Himalayan bird species, reproduced smaller in the new book.

The Birds of Travancore and Cochin 1953. Precursor to the *Birds of Kerala*.

Baker, H.R. & C.M. Inglis *Birds of Southern India* 1930. With a number of colour plates. Relies much on Stuart Baker's work.

Bates, R.S.P. & E.H.N. Lowther *Breeding Birds of Kashmir* 1952. An excellent text and many fine photographs.

Dharmakumarsinhji, R.S. *Birds of Saurashtra* 1954. A sumptuous local avifauna with many colour plates and photographs.

Fleming, R.L. & J. Bangdel *Birds of Nepal** 1976. With 150 colour plates. A good pocket guide, the only existing one to the area.

Henry, G.M. *A Guide to the Birds of Ceylon** Oxford University Press 2nd. ed. 1971. A well-illustrated and informative book; the only one available on its subject and much in demand.

Hutson, Maj. Gen. H.P.W. *The Birds about Delhi* 1954.

Inskipp, C. & T.P. *A Guide to the Birds of Nepal.* With maps for nearly all species and identification notes on difficult species and groups. Publication expected 1985.

Legge, W.V. *A History of the Birds of Ceylon* 1878–80. A historical and important treatise with 34 magnificent hand-coloured plates, by Keulemans. The only volume on Indian *(sensu lato)* birds in the splendid tradition of avifaunas and monographs published in England in the nineteenth century.

Wait, W.E. *A Manual of the Birds of Ceylon* 2nd. ed. 1931. A comprehensive textbook, now out-dated in some respects.

Textbooks or guides to birds of adjoining areas.
Etchecopar, R.D. & F. Hue. *Les Oiseaux de Chine, de Mongolie et de Coree.** Editions du Pacifique, 1978–83. A comprehensive reference work with many fine colour plates, maps and drawings. Two volumes. (In French).
Hartert, E. *Die Vogel der Palaarktischen Fauna* 3 vols. and supplement. 1903–38. A most detailed and thorough descriptive study of the birds of the Palearctic region, which borders the Oriental region along the Himalayas. (In German).
Hue, F. & R.D. Etchecopar *Les Oiseaux du Proche at du Moyen Orient** Boubee, Paris 1970. A valuable guide to the birds of the Middle East, with 32 colour plates, many maps and drawings. (In French).
King, B., M.W. Woodcock & E.C. Dickenson *A Field Guide to the Birds of South-east Asia** Collins, London. A comprehensive and fully illustrated guide to birds of continental south-east Asia. Deals with a great many birds occurring in India and the Himalayas.
Oates, E.W. *A Handbook to the Birds of British Burma* 2 vols., 1883. The first systematic work on birds of the area.
Paludan, K. *On the Birds of Afghanistan* Copenhagen 1959.
Smythies, B.E. *The Birds of Burma* 2nd. revised ed. London 1953. A detailed and comprehensive reference work. Many colour plates.
Vaurie, C. *The Birds of the Palearctic Fauna* 2 vols. 1959–65. Witherby London. An invaluable taxonomic study, with full and carefully researched details on speciation, range and status. Many of the species dealt with breed in the Himalayas; others winter in India.
*Tibet and its Birds** Witherby, London, 1972. Another careful study; the only book available on the area.

General reading.
The titles listed in this section include background reading on natural history and travel as well as those more specifically about birds. Even the most single-minded ornithologist in India cannot fail to be stirred by the richness and fascination of the flora and wild-life in general. Many of the books on exploration or plant-hunting make most interesting reading, and are valuable in setting one's study of the bird-life in a wider dimension. This is not by any means a comprehensive list, but does include many well-known titles and classics.

Adams, A.L. *Wanderings of a Naturalist in India* 1867. Written by an army surgeon, widely-travelled and interesting, with an observant eye for nature. There are many references to birds.
Baker, E.C. Stuart *The Indian Ducks and their Allies* 1908. A detailed monograph on the subject, with colour plates.
Indian Pigeons and Doves 1913. A similar treatment to the above, with 27 colour plates.
The Gamebirds of India, Burma and Ceylon 3 vols., 1921. With many colour plates. Largely based on articles originally published in the

Journal of the Bombay Natural History Society, as was the volume on Ducks.
The Nidification of Birds of the Indian Empire. 4 vols, 1932–5.

Bates, R.S.P. *Bird life in India* 1931. Interesting reading, and many photographs.

Beebe, W. *A monograph of the Pheasants* 4 vols, 1918–22. A splendid work, now very expensive and difficult to find.
Pheasants, their lives and homes 2nd ed. 1936. 2 vols in one. The beautifully written and evocative account of the lengthy field-work which preceded his monograph. Many of the colour plates are reproduced, although smaller. A fascinating book.

Blatter, E. & W.S. Millard *Some beautiful Indian Trees* Bombay

Blyth, E. *Catalogue of Birds in the Museum of the Asiatic Society* 1849. A valuable reference for the historian and taxonomist.

Bor, N.L. & M.B. Raizada *Some beautiful Indian Climbers and Shrubs*

Brandis, D. *Indian Trees* Latest reprint 1971. A comprehensive tree flora, with many drawings.

Champion, F.W. *The Jungle in sunlight and shadow* Fairly typical of the large number of books on wild-life and sport published between about 1890 and 1930.

Delacour, J. *The Pheasants of the World** Country Life, London. A definitive and systematic account of all the pheasants, with much information on habits and rearing in captivity. 32 plates.

Dewar, D. *Glimpses of Indian Birds* 1913. The same author also wrote a number of other books, including guides to the birds of the plains, Himalayan and Kashmiri birds etc. etc.

Fletcher, T.B. & C.M. Inglis *Birds of an Indian Garden* 1924.

Gee, E.P. *The Wild Life of India* Collins, London. 1964.

Gould, J.A. *A Century of Birds from the Himalaya mountains* 1832. The first of Gould's large folio works, with 80 coloured plates.
The Birds of Asia 7 vols. 1850–83, with 530 hand-coloured plates. Some of the plates from these beautiful volumes are familiar as prints, also used on table mats etc.

Gray, J.E. *Illustrations of Indian zoology.* 2 vols. 1830–35. With 202 coloured plates. A very large atlas, with plates of many species never figured before, so a valuable historical work.

Henderson, G. & A.O. Hume. *Lahore to Yarkland* 1873. An account of the natural history of the journey, with a large section on birds. This section, with its 32 hand-coloured plates by Keulemans, was reprinted and rebound on its own and issued by Hume under the title of Contribution to Indian Ornithology.

Henry, G.M. *Coloured Plates of the Birds of Ceylon* 1927. Fine water-colour portraits by a noted bird-artist of a selection of common birds, with a short text for each by W.E. Wait.

Hingston, R.W. *A naturalist in Himalaya* 1920. Mainly insects.
A Naturalist in Hindustan 1923.

Hooker, J.D. *Himalayan Journals* 2 vols. 1st. ed. 1854. Reprinted in Delhi in 1969. A classic account of exploration and botanising in the Himalayas; well worth reading.

Flora of India 7 vols. 1875–97. The standard flora, which has never been superseded, although there are a number of local floras of more recent date.

Horsfield, T. & F. Moore *Catalogue of the Birds in the Museum of the Hon. East India Company* 2 vols. 1854–58. Far more than a simple list of specimens and synonyms. It has a wealth of description and field observations culled from many sources.

Hume, Allan O. *My scrap book, or rough notes on Indian oology and and ornithology* 1869. Hume was a man of immense industry, perhaps the greatest name in Indian ornithology, by profession a busy civil servant and incidentally founder of the Indian Congress. His manuscript notes, accumulated over many years, and containing life histories of nearly 700 species, on which he hoped to write a new avifauna of India, were stolen by a servant and sold as waste paper in the bazaar. He edited the magazine Stray Feathers, writing many important papers, for its 26 year life.

The Nests and Eggs of Indian Birds 3 vols. 2nd. ed. edited by E.W. Oates 1889–90. Contains photographs of some of the leading authorities of the last century. A detailed compendium, though much early "data" on Indian oology is suspect owing to doubtful identification or provenance of collected nests and eggs.

& C.H.T. Marshall. *The Game Birds of India, Burma and Ceylon.* 3 vols. 1879-81. A good text spoilt by rather poor pictures.

Jerdon, T.C. *Illustrations of Indian Ornithology* 1843–47. 50 plates mostly of newly discovered birds from southern India, coloured by local artists. Has considerable historical and artistic interest.

Lowther, E.H.N. *A Bird photographer in India* 1949. Good reading and many photographs. The author had extensive field experience.

Lydekker, T. *The Game Animals of India,* etc. 1924. Primarily for sportsmen, it has a detailed text and many photos.

MacDonald, Malcolm. *Birds in my Indian garden* 1960. Fine photos and very readable text.

Birds in the Sun 1962. Similar but with colour photos.

Marshall, Capt. G.F.L. *Bird's Nesting in India* 1877. An interesting and early guide to nest-finding, much of it in tabular form.

Puri, G.S. *Indian Forest Ecology* 2 vols. 1960. Contains much useful background reading on plant and animal ecology. Many maps, photos, diagrams etc.

Ripley, S. Dillon *Search for the Spiny Babbler* 1952. An entertaining account of birding in Nepal.

Sharpe, R.B. *Scientific results of the Second Yarkand Mission* 1891. With 24 hand-coloured plates, mostly by Keulemans.

Smythe, F.S. *The Valley of Flowers* 1938. Botany and travel in the western Himalayas.
Stainton, J.D.A. *Forests of Nepal* 1972.
Tennent, J.E. *The Natural History of Ceylon* 1868. An early classic.
Wadia, D.N. *Geology of India* 3rd. ed. 1953.
Ward, Frank Kingdon *Assam Adventure* 1941. An account of one of this well-known author's botanical expeditions, interesting, well-written and illustrated with photos. Many of his other books concern Tibet, just outside the scope of this review.
Plant Hunter in Manipur 1952.

Journals.

Three outstandingly important journals deserve mention, two solely on birds, the other on the whole spectrum of natural history. *Stray Feathers – A Journal of Ornithology for India and its Dependencies.* Edited throughout its life by Allan Hume, it appeared in 12 volumes from 1873 to 1899, at rather irregular intervals. It contains a mass of information on Asian birds, much contributed by the Editor, but drawing contributions from all the leading names in Indian ornithology. Some of the articles are major works in their own right – volume 2, for instance, (1874), has 294 pages on the birds of the Islands of the Bay of Bengal. Volume 6 is devoted to 554 pages on the Birds of Tenasserim, by Hume. Vol. 8, (1879) has a major contribution on the Birds of Nepal, and Hume's "Rough tentative list of the Birds of India". In the last volume of text in 1899, Hume devotes 353 pages to the Birds of Manipur, Assam, Sylhet and Cachar, although by the time it was published his official duties had become so onerous that he had entirely given up the study of ornithology.

Journal of the Bombay Natural History Society. First appearing in 1886, the Journal still publishes annually, three parts making up a volume. There is such a wealth of information and illustration in this magnificent series of volumes as to eclipse any other journal in its field. The articles on birds are legion, and a major reference source. Many of the earlier volumes, which are extremely thick, have many splendid colour plates. The Journal continues to publish information on birds and is indispensable to those maintaining an interest in the ornithology of the area. The society is well worth joining – write to *Bombay Natural History Society, Hornbill House, Shahid Bhagat Singh Road, BOMBAY 400 023 India.*

The Oriental Bird Club was established in 1985 to promote the study of the birds of the region and their conservation. It has rapidly proved to be a dynamic and important force in Oriental ornithology, liaising with and promoting the work of local societies and publishing two excellent Bulletins and a fine journal *Forktail* every year. For membership details write to *Oriental Bird Club, c/o the Lodge, Sandy, Bedfordshire, SG19 2DL, U.K.*

Index

Accentor, Blackthroated 151
Rufous-breasted 151
Accipiter badius 36
trivirgatus 133
virgatus 133
Acridotheres fuscus 119
gingianus 119
tristis 119
Acrocephalus dumetorum 154
stentoreus 154
Actinodura nipalensis 105
Adjutant, Lesser 130
Adjutant Stork 23
Aegithalos concinnus 106
Aegithina tiphia 89
Aethopyga gouldiae 157
ignicauda 157
nipalensis 157
siparaja 109
Alauda gulgula 78
Alcedo atthis 72
Alcippe castaneceps 105
poioicephala 105
vinipectus 156
Alectoris chukar 45
Amandava amandava 112
formosa 112
Amaurornis fuscus 51
phoenicurus 51
Ammomanes phoenicurus 149
Ammoperdix griseogularis 135
Anas acuta 28
clypeata 131, 132
crecca 28
penelope 131, 132
platyrhynchos 131, 132
poecilorhyncha 28
querquedula 131, 132
strepera 131, 132
Anastomus oscitans 22
Anhinga rufa 16
Anser anser 130
indicus 26
Anthracoceros coronatus 146
malabaricus 146
Anthreptes singalensis 157
Anthropoides virgo 47
Anthus campestris 150
hodgsoni 149
nilghiriensis 150
novaeseelandiae 82
similis 150
trivialis 149
Apus affinis 70
melba 70
pacificus 144
Aquila rapax 35
Arachnothera longirostris 157
Arborophila rufogularis 135
torqueola 43
Ardea cinerea 19
insignis 129
purpurea 129
Ardeola grayii 21
Arenaria interpres 138
Artamus fuscus 90
Athene brama 69
Avadavat, Green 112
Red 112
Aviceda jerdoni 133
Aythya ferina 131, 132
fuligula 131, 132
nyroca 28

Babbler, Black-headed 103
Brown-capped 155
Ceylon Rufous 155
Chestnut-headed Tit- 105
Common 101
Jungle 101
Large Grey 101
Quaker 105
Red-capped 155
Rufous-bellied 103
Spotted 103
White-browed Tit- 156
White-headed 155
Yellow-breasted 103
Yellow-eyed 103
Barbet, Blue-throated 76
Crimson-throated 147
Great 147
Green 76
Lineated 147
Small Green 147
Yellow-fronted 147
Barwing, Nepal Hoary 105
Bee-Eater, Blue-bearded 146
Blue-cheeked 73, 146
Blue-tailed 73
Chestnut-headed 73
European 146
Little Green 73
Bittern, Black 129
Chestnut 129
Little 129
Yellow 20
Blackbird 94
Grey-winged 153
White-collared 153
Bluebird, Fairy 89
Bombycilla garrulus 151
Booby, Masked 126
Brainfever Bird 67
Broadbill, Collared 148
Long-tailed 148
Bubo bubo 69
coromandus 144
nipalensis 144
Buceros bicornis 75
Bubulcus ibis 19
Bulbul, Black 87
Black-crested Yellow 150
Brown-eared 150
Redvented 87
Red-whiskered 87
White-browed 87
White-cheeked 87
Yellow-browed 150
Yellow-eared 150
Bullfinch, Orange 159
Redheaded 111
Bunting, Black-faced 159
Black-headed 110
Crested 159
Redheaded 110
Rock 110
White-capped 159
Yellow-breasted 159
Burhinus oedicnemus 58
Bush-chat, Dark grey 152
Pied 96
Bush-lark, Redwinged 78
Rufous-winged 149
Singing 149
Bush-robin, Redflanked 152
Bustard, Great Indian 48
Bustard-Quail, Indian 136
Little 45
Yellow-legged 136
Butastur teesa 35
Buteo rufinus 133
Butorides striatus 21
Buzzard, Crested Honey- 133
Long-legged 133
White-eyed 35

Cacomantis merulinus 67
sonneratii 143
Calandrella cinerea 78
Calidris alba 138
alpina 138

ferruginea 138
minutus 56
Caprimulgus asiaticus 70
Carduelis carduelis 158
spinoides 111
Carpodacus erythrinus 111
Catreus wallichii 136
Centropus chlororhynchus 143
sinensis 66
toulou 143
Cercomela fusca 97
Certhia himalayana 107
Ceryle rudis 72
Ceyx erithacus 145
Chaimarrornis leucocephalus 152
Chalcophaps indica 142
Charadrius alexandrinus 54
dubius 54
leschenaultii 54
mongolus 138
Chat, Indian Blue 152
River 152
Chiffchaff, Brown 98
Chlamydotis undulata 48
Chlidonias hybrida 61
Chloropsis aurifrons 89
cochinchinensis 89
hardwickii 150
Choriotis nigriceps 48
Chrysocolaptes festivus 148
lucidus 148
Chrysomma sinense 103
Chukar 45
Ciconia ciconia 23
episcopus 23
nigra 130
Cinclus pallasii 151
Circaetus gallicus 134
Circus aeruginosus 32
macrourus 32
melanoleucos 134
Cissa chinensis 158
ornata 158
Cisticola exilis 153
juncidis 98
Clamator jacobinus 67
Collocalia brevirostris 144
unicolor 144
Columba elphinstonii 142
hodgsonii 142
leuconota 142
livia 62
torringtoni 142
Coot 51
Coppersmith 76
Copsychus malabaricus 94
saularis 94
Coracias benghalensis 75
garrulus 75, 146
Coracina melanoptera 84
novaehollandiae 84
Cormorant, Great 16
Little 17
Corvus corax 158
macrorhynchos 122
monedula 158
splendens 122
Coturnix chinensis 45
coromandelica 44
coturnix 44
Coucal 66
Ceylon 143
Lesser 143
Courser, Indian 58
Crake, Baillon's 137
Indian Banded 136
Ruddy 51
Crane, Common 47
Demoiselle 47
Sarus 46
Siberian 136
Crow, House 122
Jungle 122
Cuckoo 143
Bay-banded 143
Indian 143
Indian Plaintive 67
Large Hawk- 142
Pied Crested 67
Sirkeer 143
Cuckoo-Shrike, Black-headed 84
Large 84
Cuculus canorus 143
micropterus 143
sparverioides 142
varius 67
Culicicapa ceylonensis 92
Curlew 56
Cursorius coromandelicus 58
Cyornis tickelliae 92
Cypsiurus parvus 70

Dabchick 16
Darter 16
Delichon nipalensis 149
urbica 149
Dendrocitta formosae 158
leucogastra 158
vagabunda 121
Dendrocopos auriceps 148
himalayensis 148
mahrattensis 77
nanus 148
Dendrocygna bicolor 130
javanica 26
Dicaeum agile 109
cruentatum 157
erythrorhynchos 109
ignipectus 157
Dicrurus adsimilis 123
aeneus 157
caerulescens 123
hottentotus 157
leucophaeus 157
paradiseus 123
Dinopium benghalense 77
Dipper, Brown 151
Dove, Collared 62
Emerald 142
Little Brown 62
Red Turtle 62
Rufous Turtle 142
Spotted 62
Dromas ardeola 137, 139
Drongo, Black 123
Bronzed 157
Grey 157
Large Racket-tailed 123
Spangled 157
White-bellied 123
Drongo-Cuckoo, Indian 143
Duck, Brahminy 28
Comb 26
Ferruginous 28
Fulvous Whistling 130
Spotbill 28
Tufted 131, 132
Whistling 26
Ducula aenea 141
badia 141
Dumetia hyperythra 103
Dunlin 138
Dupetor flavicollis 129

Eagle, Black 133, 134
Crested Hawk- 36
Crested Serpent- 35
Hodgson's Hawk- 134
Pallas's Fish- 35
Short-toed 133, 134
Tawny 35
White-bellied Sea- 134
Egret, Cattle 19
Intermediate 129
Large 129
Little 19, 129
Egretta alba 129
garzetta 19
gularis 19
intermedia 129
Elanus caeruleus 32
Emberiza aureola 159
bruniceps 110
cia 110
melanocephala 110

spodocephala 159
stewarti 159
Enicurus maculatus 153
scouleri 153
Eremopterix grisea 78
nigriceps 149
Erithacus brunneus 152
cyanurus 152
Esacus recurvirostris 137
Eudynamys scolopacea 66
Eupodotis bengalensis 48
Eurystomus orientalis 146

Falco chicquera 36
jugger 36
peregrinus 135
tinnunculus 36
Falcon, Laggar 36
Shahin 135
Falconet, Redbreasted 135
Fantail, White-browed 92
White-spotted 92
Yellow-bellied 155
Ficedula nigrorufa 154
parva 92
superciliaris 154
Finch-Lark, Ashy-crowned 78
Black-crowned 149
Rufous-tailed 149
Finfoot 137
Flamingo, Greater 25
Lesser 130
Florican, Bengal 48
Flowerpecker, Fire-breasted 157
Scarlet-backed 157
Thick-billed 109
Tickell's 109
Flycatcher, Black and Orange 154
Dusky Blue 155
Grey-headed 92
Paradise 92
Red-breasted 92
Tickell's 92
Ultramarine 154
Verditer 155
Flycatcher-Shrike, Pied 150
Forktail, Little 153
Spotted 153
Francolinus francolinus 43
pictus 43
pondicerianus 43
Fregata ariel 128
Frigate-bird, Least 128
Frogmouth, Hodgson's 144
Fulica atra 51

Gadwall 131, 132
Galerida cristata 78
deva 149
malabarica 149
Gallicrex cinerea 53
Gallinago gallinago 56
stenura 138
Gallinula chloropus 51
Galloperdix bicalcarata 135
lunulata 135
spadicea 43
Gallus gallus 39
lafayetti 136
sonneratii 39
Garganey 131, 132
Garrulax albogularis 101
cinereifrons 155
delesserti 156
erythrocephalus 156
jerdoni 156
leucolophus 100
lineatus 100
pectoralis 156
Garrulus lanceolatus 158
Gelochelidon nilotica 140
Glareola lactea 58
pratincola 137
Glaucidium cuculoides 144
radiatum 69
Godwit, Bar-tailed 138
Black-tailed 138
Goldfinch, Himalayan 158
Goosander 132
Goose, Bar-headed 26
Greylag 130
Goshawk, Crested 133
Gracula ptilogenys 158
religiosa 119
Grebe, Blacknecked 125
Great Crested 125
Greenfinch, Himalayan 111
Greenshank 138
Grosbeak, Black and Yellow 158
Grus antigone 46
grus 47
leucogeranus 136
Gull, Black-headed 61
Brown-headed 61
Herring 140
Great Black-headed 140
Slender-billed 140
Gypaetus barbatus 30
Gyps benghalensis 30
himalayensis 134
indicus 30

Haematopus ostralegus 137
Halcyon chloris 145
pileata 145
smyrnensis 72
Haliaeetus leucogaster 134
leucoryphus 35
Haliastur indus 32
Harpactes fasciatus 145
Harrier, Marsh 32
Pallid 32
Pied 134
Hawk, Brown Lizard-133
Hemiprocne longipennis 70
Hemipus picatus 150
Heron, Grey 19
Little Green 21
Night 20
Purple 129
Reef 19
White-bellied 129
Heterophasia capistrata 105
Himantopus himantopus 58
Hippolais caligata 154
Hirundo concolor 81
daurica 81
fluvicola 81
rupestris 149
rustica 81
smithii 81
tahitica 149
Hoopoe, 75
Hornbill, Common Grey 75
Great Pied 75
Indian Pied 146
Malabar Grey 146
Malabar Pied 146
Houbara 48
Hydrophasianus chirurgus 53
Hypocolius ampelinus 151
Hypocolius, Grey 151
Hypsipetes flavala 150
indicus 150
madagascariensis 87

Ibidorhyncha struthersii 137
Ibis, Black 25
Glossy 24
White 24
Ibis leucocephalus 22
Ibisbill 137
Ictinaetus malayensis 134
Iora, Common 89
Irena puella 89
Ithaginis cruentus 135

Ixobrychus
cinnamomeus 129
minutus 129
sinensis 20

Jacana, Bronze-winged 53
Pheasant-tailed 53
Jackdaw 158
Jay, Black-throated 158
Junglefowl, Ceylon 136
Grey 39
Red 39
Jynx torquilla 147

Kestrel 36
Ketupa zeylonensis 69
Kingfisher, Black-capped 145
Brown-headed Stork-billed 145
Common 72
Pied 72
Three-toed 145
White-breasted 72
White-collared 145
Kite, Black-winged 32
Brahminy 32
Pariah 32
Koel 66

Lammergeyer 30
Lanius cristatus 90
excubitor 90
schach 90
vittatus 90
Lapwing, Red-wattled 54
Spur-winged 138
Yellow-wattled 54
Lark, Crested 78
Deccan Crested 149
Malabar Crested 149
Short-toed 78
Larus argentatus 140
brunnicephalus 61
genei 140
ichthyaetus 140
ridibundus 61
Laughing-Thrush, Ashy-headed 155
Black-gorgeted 156
Kerala 156
Redheaded 156
Rufous-vented 156
Streaked 100
White-crested 100
White-throated 101
Leafbird, Gold-fronted 89
Jerdon's 89
Orange-bellied 150
Leiothrix argentauris 156
lutea 105
Leptopilos dubius 23
javanicus 130
Lerwa lerwa 135
Likh 48
Limosa lapponica 138
limosa 138
Lonchura malabarica 113
malacca 113
punctulata 112
striata 113
Lophophorus impejanus 41
Lophura leucomelana 41
Loriculus beryllinus 142
vernalis 64
Lorikeet, Ceylon 142
Indian 64

Macronous gularis 103
Magpie, Ceylon Blue 158
Green 158
Red-billed Blue 121
Magpie-Robin 94
Malkoha, Redfaced 143
Small Green-billed 143
Mallard 131, 132
Martin, Crag 149
Dusky Crag 81
House 149
Nepal House 149
Plain Sand 149
Megalaima asiatica 76
flavifrons 147
haemacephala 76
lineata 147
rubricapilla 147
virens 147
viridis 147
zeylanica 76
Melophus lathami 159
Mergus merganser 132
Merlin, Red-headed 36
Merops apiaster 146
leschenaulti 73
orientalis 73
philippinus 73
superciliosus 73, 146
Mesia, Silver-eared 156
Metopidius indicus 53
Microhierax caerulescens 135
Micropternus brachyurus 147
Milvus migrans 32
Minivet, Scarlet 85
Small 85
White-bellied 150
Minla strigula 105
Mirafra assamica 149
erythroptera 78
javanica 149
Monal 41
Monarch, Black-naped 155
Monarcha azurea 155
Monticola
cinclorhynchus 152
solitarius 95
Moorhen 51
Purple 53
Motacilla alba 82
cinerea 150
citreola 82
flava 82
maderaspatensis 82
Munia, Black-headed 113
Spotted 112
White-backed 113
White-throated 113
Muscicapa sordida 155
thalassina 155
Mycerobas icterioides 158
Myiophoneus
caeruleus 94
horsfieldii 152
Myna, Bank 119
Brahminy 116
Ceylon Hill 158
Common 119
Grey-headed 116
Hill 119
Jungle 119
Pied 116

Nakta 26
Nectarinia asiatica 108
lotenia 157
zeylanica 108
Neophron percnopterus 30
Netta rufina 132
Nettapus
coromandelianus 26
Nightjar, Indian 70
Niltava, Rufous-bellied 154
Niltava sundara 154
Numenius arquata 56
phaeopus 138
Nuthatch, Chestnut-bellied 107
Velvet-fronted 107
Nycticorax nycticorax 20
Nyctiornis athertoni 146

Oceanites oceanicus 126
Oenanthe isabellina 152
picata 152
Oriole, Black-headed 121
Golden 121
Maroon 157
Oriolus oriolus 121
traillii 157
xanthornus 121
Orthotomus sutorius 98
Osprey 134
Otus bakkamoena 69

Owl, Barn 144
Brown Fish- 69
Brown Wood 144
Collared Scops 69
Dusky Horned 144
Forest Eagle- 144
Indian Eagle- 69
Mottled Wood 144
Owlet, Barred 144
Jungle 69
Spotted 69
Oystercatcher 137

Pachycephala grisola 155
Paddybird 21
Pandion haliaetus 134
Parakeet, Alexandrine 64
Blossom-headed 64
Blue-winged 142
Layard's 142
Red-breasted 142
Rose-ringed 64
Slaty-headed 142
Partridge, Black 43
Common Hill- 43
Grey 43
Painted 43
Rufous-throated Hill- 135
Seesee 135
Snow 135
Parus major 106
monticolus 156
rubidiventris 156
xanthogenys 106
Passer domesticus 115
montanus 158
rutilans 158
Pavo cristatus 39
Peafowl 39
Pelargopsis capensis 145
Pelecanus crispus 127
onocrotalus 127
philippensis 128
Pelican, Dalmatian 127
Spot-billed 127, 128
White 127
Pellorneum fuscocapillum 155
ruficeps 103
Perdicula asiatica 45
erythrorhyncha 135
Pericrocotus cinnamomeus 85
erythropygius 150
flammeus 85
Pernis ptilorhynchus 133
Petronia xanthocollis 115
Phaenicophaeus pyrrhocephalus 143
Phaethon aethereus 126
Phalacrocorax carbo 16
fuscicollis 16
niger 17
Pheasant, Blood 135
Chir 136
Kalij 41
Koklas 136
Philomachus pugnax 138
Phoenicopterus minor 130
ruber 25
Phoenicurus ochruros 97
Phylloscopus affinis 154
collybita 98
inornatus 154
occipitalis 154
Piculet, Speckled 147
Picumnus innominatus 147
Picus canus 147
chlorolophus 147
myrmecophoneus 147
Pigeon, Blue Rock 62
Ceylon Wood 142
Green 62
Green Imperial 141
Grey-fronted Green 141
Maroon-backed Imperial 141
Nilgiri Wood 142
Orange-breasted Green 141
Snow 142
Speckled Wood 142
Pintail 28
Pipit, Brown Rock 150
Indian 82
Indian Tree 149
Nilgiri 150
Tawny 150
Tree 149
Pitta brachyura 78
sordida 148
Pitta, Hooded 148
Indian 78
Platalea leucorodia 24
Plegadis falcinellus 24
Ploceus benghalensis 115
manyar 115
philippinus 115
Plover, Crab 137, 139
Great Sand 54
Grey 138
Kentish 54
Lesser Golden 54
Lesser Sand 138
Little Ringed 54
Pluvialis dominica 54
squatarola 138
Pochard 131, 132
Red-crested 132
Podiceps cristatus 125
nigricollis 125
Pomatorhinus schisticeps 103
Porphyrio porphyrio 53
Porzana pusilla 137
Pratincole, Large Indian 137
Little 58
Prinia, Ashy 98
Grey-breasted 153
Indian 98
Jungle 98
Rufous-fronted 154
Prinia buchanani 154
criniger 98
hodgsonii 153
socialis 98
subflava 98
sylvatica 154
Prunella atrogularis 151
strophiata 151
Psarisomus dalhousiae 148
Pseudibis papillosa 25
Psittacula alexandri 142
calthorpae 142
columboides 142
cyanocephala 64
eupatria 64
himalayana 142
krameri 64
Pterocles exustus 58
indicus 141
Pucrasia macrolopha 136
Puffinus pacificus 126
Pycnonotus cafer 87
jocosus 87
leucogenys 87
luteolus 87
melanicterus 150
penicillatus 150
Pyrrhula aurantiaca 159
erythrocephala 111

Quail, Blue-breasted 45
Common 44
Jungle Bush- 45
Painted Bush- 135
Rain 44

Rail, Slaty-breasted 51
Rallina eurizonoides 136
Rallus striatus 51
Raven 158
Redshank 138
Redstart, Black 97
Plumbeous 97
Rhipidura albogularis 92
aureola 92
hypoxantha 155
Rhopocichla atriceps 103
Rhopodytes viridirostris 143

Rhyacornis fuliginosus 97
Riparia paludicola 149
Robin, Indian 96
Pekin 105
Rock-chat, Brown 97
Roller, Broad-billed 146
Indian 75
Kashmir 75, 146
Rosefinch, Common 111
Rostratula benghalensis 53
Rubycheek 157
Ruff 138
Rynchops albicollis 141

Sanderling 138
Sandgrouse, Chestnut-bellied 58
Painted 141
Sandpiper, Common 56
Curlew- 138
Wood 56
Sarkidiornis melanotos 26
Saxicola caprata 96
ferrea 152
torquata 96
Saxicoloides fulicata 96
Scimitar-Babbler, Slaty-headed 103
Seicercus xanthoschistos 98
Serilophus lunatus 148
Shag, Indian 16
Shama 94
Shearwater, Wedge-tailed 126
Shelduck, Common 130
Shikra 36
Shoveler 131, 132
Shrike, Bay-backed 90
Brown 90
Indian Grey 90
Rufous-backed 90
Sibia, Black-headed 105
Sitta castanea 107
frontalis 107
Siva, Bar-throated 105
Skimmer, Indian 141
Skua, Arctic 140
Skylark, Small 78
Snipe, Common 56
Painted 53
Pintail 138
Sparrow, Cinnamon-Tree- 158
House 115
Tree 158
Yellow-throated 115
Sparrowhawk, Besra 133
Spiderhunter, Little 157
Spilornis cheela 35
Spizaetus cirrhatus 36
nipalensis 134
Spoonbill 24
Spotbill 28
Spurfowl, Ceylon 135
Painted 135
Red 43
Starling, Common 116
Rosy 116
Stercorarius parasiticus 140
Sterna acuticauda 61
albifrons 141
aurantia 61
bengalensis 141
bergii 141
caspia 141
Stilt, Black-winged 58
Stint, Little 56
Stonechat 96
Stone Curlew 58
Great 137
Stork, Adjutant 23
Black 130
Black-necked 130
Lesser Adjutant 130
Openbill 22
Painted 22
White 23
White-necked 23
Storm-Petrel, Wilson's 126
Streptopelia chinensis 62
decaocto 62
orientalis 142
senegalensis 62
tranquebarica 62
Strix leptogrammica 144
ocellata 144
Sturnus contra 116
malabaricus 116
pagodarum 116
roseus 116
vulgaris 116
Sula dactylatra 126
Sunbird, Fire-tailed 157
Green-tailed 157
Maroon-breasted 157
Mrs. Gould's 157
Purple 108
Purple-rumped 108
Yellow-backed 109
Surniculus lugubris 143
Swallow, Cliff 81
Common 81
House 149
Red-rumped 81
Wire-tailed 81
Swallow-Shrike, Ashy 90
Swift, Alpine 70
Crested Tree- 70
House 70
Palm 70
White-rumped 144
Swiftlet, Edible-nest 144
Himalayan 144
Sypheotides indica 48
Taccocua leschenaulti 143
Tachybaptus ruficollis 16
Tadorna ferruginea 28
tadorna 130, 131
Tailorbird 98
Teal, Common 28
Cotton 26
Tephrodornis pondicerianus 85
Tern, Black-bellied 61
Caspian 141
Gull-billed 140
Indian River 61
Lesser Crested 141
Little 141
Swift 141
Whiskered 61
Terpsiphone paradisi 92
Threskiornis melanocephalus 24
Thrush, Black-throated 153
Blue Rock- 95
Blue-headed Rock- 152
Malabar Whistling 152
Orange-headed Ground 152
Plain-backed Mountain 152
Spotted-winged Ground 152
Tickell's 153
Whistling 94
White's 152
Timalia pileata 155
Tit, Black 156
Green-backed 156
Grey 106
Red-headed 106
Yellow-cheeked 106
Tockus birostris 75
griseus 146
Torgos calvus 30
Tragopan melanocephalus 135
satyra 41
Tragopan, Satyr 41
Western 135
Tree-Creeper, Himalayan 107
Tree-Pie, Himalayan 158
Indian 121
White-bellied 158
Treron bicincta 141
phoenicoptera 62
pompadora 141
Tringa glareola 56
hypoleucos 56
nebularia 138
totanus 138
Troglodytes troglodytes 151
Trogon, Indian 45

Tropicbird, Redbilled 126
Turdoides affinis 155
caudatus 101
malcolmi 101
rufescens 155
striatus 101
Turdus albocinctus 153
boulboul 153
merula 94
ruficollis 153
unicolor 153
Turnix suscitator 136
sylvatica 45
tanki 136
Turnstone 138
Tyto alba 144

Upupa epops 75
Urocissa erythrorhyncha 121

Vanellus indicus 54
malabaricus 54
spinosus 138
Vulture, Himalayan Griffon 134
King 30
Long-billed 30
Scavenger 30
White-backed 30

Wagtail, Grey 150
Large Pied 82
White 82
Yellow 82
Yellow-headed 82
Warbler, Blyth's Reed 154
Booted 154
Brown Hill- 98
Clamorous 154
Crowned Leaf- 154
Grey-headed Flycatcher- 98
Red-headed Fantail- 153
Streaked Fantail- 98
Tickell's Leaf- 154
Yellow-browed Leaf- 154
Watercock 53
Waterhen, White-breasted 51
Waxwing 151
Weaver, Baya 115
Black-throated 115
Streaked 115
Wheater, Isabelline 152
Pied 152
Whimbrel 138
Whistler, Mangrove 155
White-eye, Indian 108
Wigeon 131, 132
Woodpecker, Black-backed 148
Black-naped Green 147
Brown-crowned Pygmy 148
Brown-fronted Pied 148
Golden-backed 77
Kashmir Pied 148
Large Golden-backed 148
Little Scaly-bellied Green 147
Mahratta 77
Rufous 147
Small Yellow-naped 147
Wood-Shrike, Common 85
Wren 151
Wryneck 147

Xenorhynchus asiaticus 130

Yuhina flavicollis 105
gularis 156
Yuhina, Stripe-throated 156
Yellow-naped 105

Zoothera dauma 152
citrina 152
mollissima 152
spiloptera 152
Zosterops palpebrosa 108